THE BEAD  JEWELLERY BIBLE

THE BEAD JEWELLERY BIBLE

Dorothy Wood

D&C

David and Charles

www.rucraft.co.uk

A DAVID & CHARLES BOOK
© F&W Media International LTD 2011

David & Charles is an imprint of F&W Media International LTD
Brunel House, Forde Close, Newton Abbot, TQ12 4PU, UK

F&W Media International LTD is a subsidiary of F+W Media, Inc.
4700 East Galbraith Road, Cincinnati, OH 45236

First published in the UK & US in 2011

Text and designs copyright © Dorothy Wood 2011
Photography and illustrations © F&W Media International
LTD 2011

Dorothy Wood has asserted her right to be identified as
author of this work in accordance with the Copyright,
Designs and Patents Act, 1988.

A catalogue record for this book is available from the
British Library.

ISBN-13: 978-0-7153-3870-4 paperback
ISBN-10: 0-7153-3870-6 paperback

Printed in China by RR Donnelley
for F&W Media International LTDBrunel House, Forde Close,
Newton Abbot, TQ12 4PU, UK

10 9 8 7 6 5 4 3 2 1

Publisher Alison Myer
Acquisitions Editor Cheryl Brown
Editor James Brooks
Project Editor Cathy Joseph
Senior Designer Mia Trenoweth
Production Manager Bev Richardson
Photography Simon Whitmore

F+W Media publishes high quality books on a wide range
of subjects. For more great book ideas visit: **www.rucraft.co.uk**

Contents

Introduction

Jewellery making is a most rewarding craft. It allows you to be creative and develop skills quickly and easily to make a wide range of designs using beads and materials that are exactly to your budget, taste and style. Whether your aim is to have a hobby or to sell commercially, it is essential to know the fundamental skills of jewellery making so that the designs look professional and, crucially, don't fall apart when worn.

Jewellery design is always evolving; as fashions change, styles are created to suit new trends and popular colour schemes. This link to fashion encourages manufacturers to bring out new beads and components, providing us with greater choice for our designs.

Nevertheless, many styles of jewellery and particular techniques are timeless and the basic skills required for making a classic necklace or up-to-the-minute design are exactly the same. This book is an encyclopedia of beading information, which aims to pass on the knowledge, skills and techniques that will benefit anyone who wants to make their own jewellery. It is designed, in the first instance, to be a workbook with step-by-step instructions on all the basic techniques, and also to be a source of ideas and inspiration, giving you the opportunity to advance your skills.

The book has introductory chapters giving useful information on beads, their sizes, shapes and finishes; a guide to the principles of colour and design; basic essentials and specialist materials and tools, and an in-depth look at the vast array of findings now available to help you create fabulous designs.

There are four chapters that focus on the most popular jewellery techniques – stringing, wirework, bead stitching and bead embroidery. Each chapter gives a good grounding in the basic techniques but also shows ways to develop these skills to a more advanced level. To make the instructions as clear and easy to follow as possible, these are illustrated with step-by-step photography and diagrams. Throughout the chapters there are fabulous, inspirational projects allowing you to make pieces of jewellery straight away.

Finally there is a chapter on making your own beads, charms and pendants using a variety of different materials such as paper, fabric and clay. These beginners' guides give an understanding of the principles required to make unique beads and components for your own jewellery designs.

Beads

Much of the fun of making your own jewellery comes from choosing the ideal beads for your design and to make this as easy as possible it is worth learning a little about them. This chapter looks at shapes and sizes, storing and sorting, large and small beads and the kind of alternatives that will really make your projects stand out.

Basics

An understanding of how beads are measured and formed is especially essential if you are ordering your beads online. Once you start to build up your stash, sorting and storing them effectively is key.

BEAD SHAPES

Beads come in many different shapes and within each shape group there is further variety. For example, round beads are not only smooth, they can be facetted, grooved or fluted; bicones can be short or elongated; drops can range from leaves to dagger shape and tabular beads, which are thin flat beads, can be any shape at all.

Bicone · Rondelle · Flat square · Tear drop (top drilled)

Cylinder · Lantern · Diamond · Leaf

Oval · Nugget · Cushion · Dagger

Dice · Round · Coin · D shape (top drilled)

Cube · Drop · Lentil (drilled to overlap)

*Some beads like this **donut** have larger holes and become more like rings. Donuts can be used as connectors or pendants.*

BEAD HOLES

Most bead holes are in the centre, either vertical or horizontal, but you do get holes off-centre, going through the back like a button with a shank, or at one end. Drop beads have a hole going vertically through the bead or across the top so that the bead hangs down attractively and lentil beads have off-set holes so that the beads overlap.

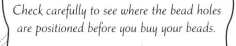

Check carefully to see where the bead holes are positioned before you buy your beads.

***Pandoro style beads** are made to fit over a thick cord or metal chain and have a very large hole.*

SORTING BEADS

Before you decide which storage to use, consider how to sort your beads. They can be stored according to their size, colour, shape or material – different types of beads lend themselves to being sorted in particular ways. For example, seed beads may be best sorted by size because that is what you select first; then you can search for a particular colour amongst your sizes. Jewellery using crystals, pearls and semi-precious beads generally uses a particular shape of bead, so they could be stored by type, whereas small quantities of large beads can be sorted by colour.

*One of the most inspiring ways to **sort beads** is by colour so you can experiment with colour schemes and create interesting mosaic jewellery.*

*Clear **screw-top containers** that stack together or tubes with secure tops are useful for small quantities of tiny beads.*

STORAGE

You are more likely to use beads from your stash if they are properly stored and easily accessible. Many beads come ready-packed in bags, tubes or packets and these may be suitable for storing beads long-term, so long as they can be opened easily and closed securely. Label beads, especially seed beads, carefully before storing in case you need to re-order in the future. You will need to record the code number, colour, size and where you bought them.

Large Beads

The assortment of large beads available for jewellery making can be overwhelming so it is a good idea to learn a little about the different styles and types before you make a selection. There are two main categories, man-made and natural, but within these two groups there is a huge variety of colours, shapes, quality and price to choose from.

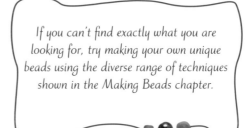

If you can't find exactly what you are looking for, try making your own unique beads using the diverse range of techniques shown in the Making Beads chapter.

GLASS

Glass is the most versatile of all beads, available in many different shapes and sizes, from transparent to opaque, with a huge range of surface and hole-lined finishes – the choice is almost infinite.

• Pressed glass beads are made in moulds to create a range of shapes, from leaves and flowers to discs, cylinders and drops.

• Czech firepolish beads are high quality faceted beads made from moulded glass; an additional torch treatment is applied to smooth visible seams and rough spots for a clean, glossy surface.

• Millefiori beads are made from canes of glass in the same way as seaside rock, and then cut into slices to reveal the decorative cross section.

• Blown glass beads are hollow and so very lightweight. They are available in stunning patterns and colours and look particularly attractive in a heart-shaped pendant bead.

LAMPWORK

These exquisite glass beads are handmade using a blowtorch, with rods or canes of plain or patterned glass, so although you can repeat the exact process, no two beads will be identical. Equipped with the right tools and equipment, it is possible to make these beads at home.

• The craft of lampwork has boomed in recent years, so there are lots of contemporary styles to choose from.

• The base bead is formed around a revolving metal rod or mandrel that determines the size of the hole.

• The bead can be decorated with extra glass and shaped using a variety of techniques.

• Top-quality Venetian lampwork beads from Murano often have metal foil linings that sparkle through the transparent glass.

*Each **lampwork bead** will have its own individual character and, when used in quantity, simple stringing can work best.*

CRYSTALS

The term 'crystal' describes a faceted bead made from cut glass but it is often used to describe inexpensive moulded glass or even faceted plastic beads.

- The quantity and precision of the cutting determines the quality of sparkle.
- Facets can be cut in different styles, such as brilliant or rivoli, for example, to create specific effects and add variety.
- Crystals can have a mirror-finish foil backing on the reverse side to enhance their brilliance.
- Fancy stones or cabochon-style crystals can be inserted into metal settings and incorporated into jewellery designs.

PEARLS

It is easy to distinguish between real and fake pearls: if you rub a real pearl against your tooth it produces a grating sensation, whereas the surface of imitation pearls is completely smooth.

- Real pearls, which also fall into the organic group, can either be cultured (from a pearl farm) or harvested from the wild.
- As with every other type of bead, the price of pearls varies with the quality – the most valuable pearls have an iridescent lustre and are not too wrinkled.
- Pearl beads have the gorgeous lustre applied to a glass bead. These are available in a range of fashion colours rather than the usual white, cream or pastel shades.
- Pearl beads, available in a range of shapes, can be quite large and they are ideal for contemporary necklaces.

*The sparkling cut facets of these Swarovski **crystal beads** are enhanced by the Aurore Boreale finish, which creates an attractive rainbow effect.*

***Pearl beads** are available in a range of fashion colours. Here, vivid lime and raspberry pearls are spaced with matching seed beads.*

METAL

Metal beads are available in a wide range of metals and alloys such as brass, copper and aluminium and different alloys as well as precious metals like silver and gold.

• Solid metal beads can be rather heavy, but hollow beads or even plastic beads with a metallic finish, are much lighter and these can be useful for long necklaces or bulky jewellery.

• Metal beads can be moulded, modelled or shaped from sheet metal. Surface finishes and patinas can add an antique or vintage look.

• Plated metal beads are not as stable as solid metal beads and the surface coating can rub off to reveal the base metal.

• Fine silver (99.9% pure) is too soft to make beads, so other metals such as copper are added to make Sterling or Bali silver (92.5% pure).

MODELLED BEADS

Common materials for mass-produced or home-made modelled beads (see the Making Beads chapter) include resin, gesso, lacquer, papier maché, ceramic, polymer clay and cinnabar.

• Polymer clay is a heat-setting clay available in a wide range of intermixable colours. The clay can be rolled, shaped or moulded.

• Ceramic beads can have a matt or glazed finish. They are baked in a kiln and, just like crockery, are prone to breaking or chipping on hard surfaces.

• Wet felting using wool fibres is an easy way to make large, lightweight beads, and these can be embellished further with seed beads.

• Paper can be used to make a variety of beads either by rolling strips or by moulding papier mâché. The surface must be sealed with varnish or paint.

PLASTIC

These beads range from cheap and cheerful to the highly collectable early bakelite and vulcanite beads. More recent plastics include perspex, acetate and coloured cast resins.

• Plastic beads can be anything from clear to opaque and they are available in a huge range of colours. As these beads are moulded they can be made in almost any shape or size.

• Lucite beads are delightful, translucent, frosted flowers and leaves that look quite realistic and are extremely light.

• Plastic beads can be dyed or coated with metallic finishes that look surprisingly authentic but have the advantage of being much lighter than metal beads.

• Epoxy resin beads, formed by mixing two materials that react together to create a solid bead, can be made to almost any shape or size.

Metal beads are available in all shapes and sizes but, when stringing several together in your design, do choose hollow ones otherwise the necklace may end up too heavy to be worn.

GEMSTONES

Gemstone beads are pieces of semi-precious mineral that have been cut and polished to make extremely attractive and valuable beads. Often sold in strings, the price varies considerably depending on the aesthetic value and rarity of the mineral.

• Some rocks, such as lapis lazuli, and organic materials like amber or jet are considered to be gemstones too.

• Transparent gemstones are sometimes faceted to add sparkle, and opaque gemstones like opal are often made into cabochons.

• Some semi-precious stones, such as jade, are dyed to produce a more varied range of colours.

• Inexpensive chips are small, rough pieces of mineral that look stunning when crocheted with wire.

ORGANIC

Made from a huge variety of natural materials, such as seeds, nuts, shells, bones, coral and horn, organic beads were the first beads made by our ancestors for artistic ornamentation and they are still just as popular today.

• Pearls and certain semi-precious beads, formed from plant or animal material, can also be classed as organic.

• Some organic materials, ivory, amber, tortoiseshell and jet included, are now rare, but can be found in vintage jewellery.

• Painted wood beads are pretty and cheap, but look out also for attractive beads made from unusual woods from around the world.

• Go foraging for your own organic beads – look in woodland for seeds and nuts, and on the beach for shells, small pieces of driftwood and pieces of tumbled glass that can be incorporated into your jewellery projects.

*A cluster of **frosted resin** flower and leaf-shaped beads in an array of pastel shades are made extra-special with the addition of ivory-pearl bead centres.*

*Beads made from **bone and wood** complement each other beautifully. Look out for carved and painted beads for extra interest.*

*The **onyx and agate beads** used in this necklace are both forms of the semi-precious mineral quartz. They contrast beautifully with the silver beads and heart charm in this simple necklace design.*

Small Beads

Often known generically as seed beads, these small beads may all look the same at first glance but there are wide variations in shape, size, finish and quality. Small beads are generally sold for bead stitching but are useful for spacing larger beads and elongating necklaces without adding weight. The most common types of small beads are listed below.

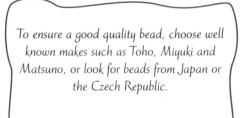

To ensure a good quality bead, choose well known makes such as Toho, Miyuki and Matsuno, or look for beads from Japan or the Czech Republic.

SEED BEADS

These round, doughnut-shaped beads, also known as rocailles, range from size 3 to 15 – the most popular is 11. Larger seed beads are known as pebble or pony beads and the smaller ones are known as petites.

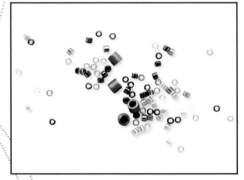

CYLINDER BEADS

Also known by their trade names Delicas, Antiques or Magnificas, these precision-milled, tubular beads have a large hole enabling you to pass the thread through each bead several times. They are ideal for bead stitching because of their uniform size. Look out for double Delicas, which are much larger and available smooth or with a hex finish.

HEX BEADS

These are cylindrical beads made from a six-sided glass cane and are like a squat bugle bead (see Bugles). Satin beads and twisted hex beads (also know as two-cuts), are similar in shape and also useful for creating texture alongside smooth seed beads.

MAGATAMAS

Originally comma shaped, these small beads are now usually shaped like a squat drop bead with an off-centre hole. They add movement and interest when strung together or with other beads.

CHARLOTTES

These high quality seed beads from the Czech Republic have a single cut facet to make them sparkle and are much sought after. Originally charlottes were only available in size 13 but other sizes from 15 to 6 are now available, though these are more correctly known as true-cuts.

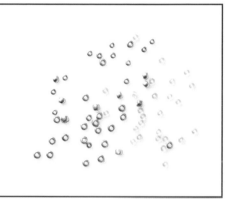

*Multiple strings of different sized **seed beads** can be plaited into a thick rope.*

*String seed beads on to fine **elastic thread** and hide the knots inside some larger beads.*

TRIANGLE BEADS

These have three sides and add an interesting texture to beaded fabric, especially herringbone stitch. There are two main styles both from Japan, the geometric sharp-sided Toho triangle and the more rounded Miyuki triangle.

PAPILLON BEADS

Also known as peanut beads, these are a new style of small bead that look like little butterfly wings, hence the name from the French word for butterfly. Because of their shape, the beads sit haphazardly when strung and add an unusual texture to designs.

BUGLES

Glass canes cut to a variety of lengths. The most common sizes are 3–4mm, 6–7mm, 9mm and 15mm. Bugles can be matched to seed beads: the smallest bugles are the same size as size 12 seed beads and the others match size 11. Twisted bugles are five- or six-sided tubes that were twisted while the glass was hot.

*Work long fringe strands out from a centre core to create a fabulous **textural bracelet**.*

SMALL BEADS SIZES

Seed beads and other tiny beads are measured in either millimetres or 'aughts', written as 11/00 for example, but more commonly known as size 11. This relates to the number of seed beads that fit into 2.5cm (1in) when laid out like a row of doughnuts. The sizes vary between the different manufacturers but, as shown below, each aught size also has a corresponding size in millimetres.

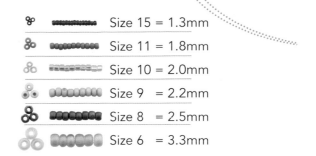

Size 15 = 1.3mm
Size 11 = 1.8mm
Size 10 = 2.0mm
Size 9 = 2.2mm
Size 8 = 2.5mm
Size 6 = 3.3mm

STONE SIZES

Small, no-hole crystals with pointed or flat backs, also known as rhinestones, have their own sizing systems known as 'ss' (stone size) and 'pp' (pearl plate). PP was the original size guide, where pearls fell through a grid of holes in different sizes to land on plates, hence 'pearl plates'. Jewellers developed their own sizing guide, 'ss' or stone size, based on a similar principle. Swarovski, which produces high quality crystals, use these sizing systems as its stones are so accurately cut. Here is a conversion chart for some common crystal sizes, rounded to the nearest whole number. PP sizes are only used up to about 4mm.

SS 5 (PP 12) 1.8mm
SS 6 (PP 14) 2mm
SS 8 (PP 18) 3mm
SS 10 (PP 22) 4mm
SS 12 3.1mm
SS 16 3.9mm

SS 20 4.7mm
SS 25 5.5mm
SS 30 6.4mm
SS 34 7mm

LARGE BEAD SIZES

Large beads are generally measured in millimetres and, depending on the shape, either have one measurement or two. Regular shapes such as round and square beads are measured once, across the diameter or the distance between the two holes, whereas most other bead shapes are measured by length and width. The first measurement is usually the distance between the bead holes, generally the length; the second measurement is usually the width (the shorter measurement).

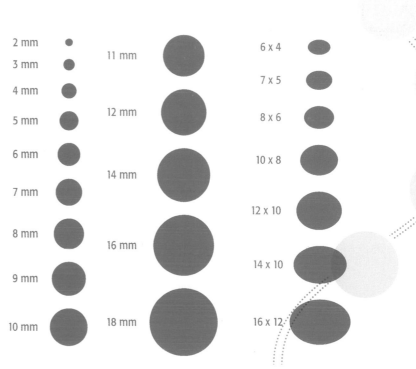

2 mm
3 mm
4 mm
5 mm
6 mm
7 mm
8 mm
9 mm
10 mm

11 mm
12 mm
14 mm
16 mm
18 mm

6 x 4
7 x 5
8 x 6
10 x 8
12 x 10
14 x 10
16 x 12

This chart is a guide to the actual size of common bead measurements but check which direction the hole is lying when ordering beads as some, such as briolettes and disc beads, have holes running across the shortest measurement.

Finishes

The huge variety of beads, especially those made from glass, stems from the wide range of finishes available. When buying beads, especially online or from a catalogue, it helps to know the terms commonly used to describe exactly what the bead looks like. For example 'SL purple AB' is a silver-lined, purple bead with an iridescent, rainbow effect on the surface ('AB' meaning aurora borealis).

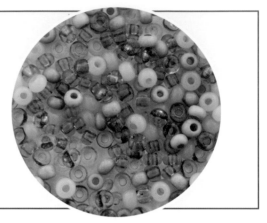

- **Transparent** beads made from clear or coloured glass are see-through, allowing the passage of light.
- **Opaque** beads have a solid colour that doesn't allow any light to pass through.
- **Translucent** beads are between transparent and opaque and are sometimes known as **greasy, opal** or **satin** beads.

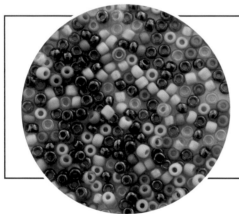

- **Gloss** beads are very shiny like glass.
- **Matt** beads are opaque beads that have been tumbled or dipped in acid to give them a dull, flat surface.
- **Frosted** beads are transparent or translucent beads that have been treated in a similar way to matt beads.

- **Dyed** beads have been painted with a dye or paint on the surface. They often have bright or unusual colours, but the dye or paint can wear off in use.

- **Colour-lined** or **inside colour** beads are transparent with the hole lined in another opaque colour.
- **Silver-lined (rocaille)** beads have the hole lined with silver and look really sparkly. Sometimes the hole is square to enhance the shine. They are also available with a matt finish that has a frosted appearance.

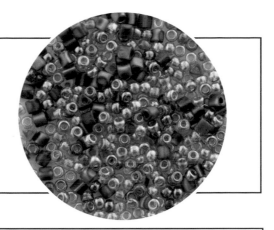

- **Iris, iridescent, rainbow** or **AB** beads have been treated with metal salts while the glass is hot to create a coating that resembles an oil slick. On matt beads, this can produce an appearance like raku or pottery-fired clay.

- **Lustre** beads are opaque beads with a coating that gives the bead a pearl finish.
- **Ceylon** beads are transparent with a milky lustre.
- **Gold** or silver **lustre** beads have been treated with a gold or silver pearl finish.

- **Metallic** beads have been heated and sprayed with oxidized tin.
- **Higher metallic** beads are surface-coated with gold and then sprayed with oxidized titanium, the gold creating a brighter finish.
- **Galvanized** beads are electroplated with zinc and have a more durable finish.

*When using beads in similar shades and in a single stitch, such as tubular herringbone, you can add interest with a mix of **gloss** and **matt** beads.*

*When creating beaded beads to work alongside other beads in a necklace, it is best to choose seed beads with **similar finishes** to the larger beads.*

Bead Alternatives

Making your own jewellery is one of the most rewarding crafts and with just a little skill you can make stunning pieces for yourself, for friends and relatives or to sell. Beads will always be the main component of most pieces of jewellery but to make something personal you can incorporate other small elements.

CHARMS

These small, usually metallic, objects with a hole or ring to hang are generally used as accents rather than focal points in jewellery. They are available in a range of metals including gold and silver.

Crystal buttons can work beautifully with beads in your jewellery.

PENDANTS

Usually larger than charms, pendants are often the focal point of a piece of jewellery. They are available in a wide range of materials. Look for antique pendants in ivory or tortoiseshell in antique or bric-a-brac shops.

BUTTONS

All sorts of buttons, from plastic to mother of pearl, can be incorporated into jewellery alongside your beads, or you can make the entire design in buttons. Even quality bead companies such as Swarovski have a wide range of crystal buttons.

*Look out for **pendants**, which can be found in a wide range of materials, to use as the focal point for a piece.*

SHELLS

Walk along any beach and you are sure to pick up an assortment of shells and tumbled glass to take home. Choose pieces with natural holes or drill tiny holes to incorporate into jewellery. Use wire wrapping to attach a piece that has no holes.

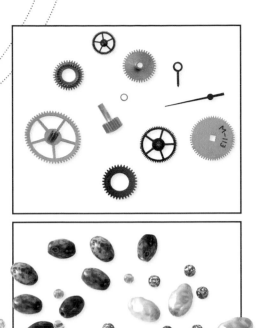

BRIC-A-BRAC
Small metallic components from the inside of old watches, such as cog wheels or even watch faces, can be incorporated into jewellery. These elements, combined with antique-looking chain or filigree stampings, are used in contemporary Steam Punk jewellery inspired by the Victorian industrial revolution.

VINTAGE BEADS
One of the most cost effective ways to collect beads and beading findings is by recycling them from jewellery that is out of date, old fashioned or damaged. Vintage is generally defined as anything over 25 years old but something labelled as 'vintage style' can merely look old. Antique pieces, on the other hand, should be over 100 years old.

IDENTIFYING VINTAGE BEADS
Before you buy a piece of second-hand jewellery, try to assess the beads to see if it is value for money. If you like the beads that is a bonus as you are likely to use them regardless but it helps to identify the material the beads are made from. Even if the beads are unattractive or damaged, you may find that the findings are suitable for use in another piece. With a little research you may also be able to ascertain from the style of the jewellery how old it is.

- Beads with an obvious seam may be moulded plastic or pressed glass.
- If the beads are warm to the touch and lightweight they are likely to be plastic rather than glass, but could be a vintage plastic such as Bakelite.
- Beware of strings of plastic beads that are moulded to the string as they will be difficult to reuse.
- Glass or gemstone beads feel cold, are relatively heavy and clink together when lifted.
- Examine jewellery carefully to see if facetted beads or crystals are chipped or damaged.
- Diamante settings can be repaired by replacing any of the missing foil-backed crystals.
- Check metal findings and beads to see if the plating is wearing off. If the beads are lightweight they may be plastic or if heavy could be solid metal.
- Look out for organic materials such as tortoiseshell and ivory, which are no longer allowed to be made into beads.

Colour and Design

Colour theory is a complex science but learning even a little of this fascinating subject will help you recognise which colours go together in perfect harmony. This chapter also looks at how to embark on your own designs using established concepts and the inspiration you have gathered from various sources.

Creating with Colour

The traditional artist's colour wheel shows how different colours are mixed. Based on the three primary colours, three secondary colours and six tertiary colours, the range can be extended to 36 colours with tints and shades in each colour. Tints are made by adding white to the base colour it and darker shades by adding black.

*Use the **colour wheel** to create some of the harmonious schemes described below.*

COLOUR SCHEMES

These harmonious schemes are based on sound colour theory and within these parameters there are innumerable variations you can create. A monochrome scheme can be created with any colour on the wheel, analogous schemes can be either cool or warm and you can modify triad schemes by changing the spacing between the colours. So get out your bead stash, experiment and have fun!

*Add shiny silver beads to matt black and grey semi-precious beads to create stunning **monochromatic** jewellery.*

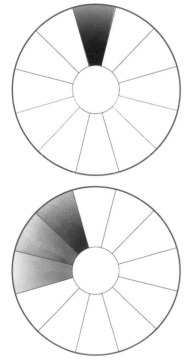

Monochromatic colour schemes look clean and elegant.
• They are very easy on the eyes, especially in blues or greens.
• Choose one colour and then paler tints and darker shades of the same colour.
• This scheme always looks balanced and visually appealing but is rarely vibrant.

Analogous colour schemes use adjacent colours on the wheel.
• They are often referred to as 'cool colours' or 'warm colours'.
• They have a richer appearance than monochromatic schemes.
• Choose one dominant colour and another one or two as accents.

*Most people find **analogous** colour schemes, like the warm reds and browns from this necklace easy to create as the colours sit next to one another on the colour chart.*

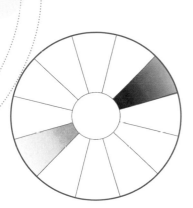

Complementary colour schemes use colours opposite one another on the colour wheel.
- Use equal quantities of each colour for a strong contrast.
- This scheme works best with a cool colour such as green/blue against a warm red, for example.
- For a subtle effect choose one main colour and use the other as an accent.

*Although there is a mixture of different colours, this crystal-encrusted bead works on the **complementary** principle.*

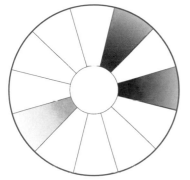

Split complementary is subtler than straight complementary colour schemes.
- Choose one colour and two colours that sit either side of its complementary colour.
- Use a single warm colour and several cool colours or vice versa.
- It works best with careful balance – one dominant, one secondary and one accent.

Triad colour schemes use three colours equally spaced around the colour wheel.
- It creates strong contrasts and richness while still retaining a balanced effect.
- Secondary triads can be surprisingly distinctive; tertiary triads contemporary and stylish.
- If the beads look gaudy, tone the colours down slightly.

Modified triads have three colours spaced on one side of the colour wheel rather than equally spaced; similar to an analogous scheme but with more impact as there is greater contrast between the colours.

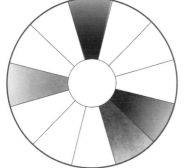

Tetrad colour schemes use two colours and their complementary colours.
- One of the most vibrant schemes using more variety of colours.
- It can be difficult to balance harmoniously.
- For best results choose one colour to be dominant or tone down the colours.

*When selecting your beads, it may help to start with a **multicoloured bead** and then choose other beads that match the various colours. In this mosaic necklace, the addition of shiny gold lifts the colours and adds a little zing.*

Colour Inspiration

Learning to use colour in clever and exciting ways is a process that requires passion, commitment and a depth of personal expression. Finding your creativity through colour is an inspirational journey; there are no specific paths, simply lots of different ways to absorb the knowledge and understanding.

SYMBOLISM OF COLOUR

Symbolism is a way of communicating a message or representing something important to you and a particular colour scheme can become powerfully symbolic in different situations. Whether it is showing patriotism or religious beliefs, or even just dressing brightly to give yourself a lift, colours can trigger strong emotions. Colours are also influenced by culture and traditions and have different connotations in countries around the world. For example, red means purity in India, it symbolises anger and aggression in the West but is a sign of sacrifice and sin in Hebrew.

BIRTHSTONES

Some gemstones, either precious or semi-precious, have become associated with particular months of the year. This is the modern list, adopted in 1912, which you can use to design very personal jewellery for someone's birthday or other special occasions. Some people believe that these stones have heightened powers during the birthday month.

JANUARY – GARNET
guidance and constancy.

FEBRUARY – AMETHYST
peace and tranquillity.

MARCH – AQUAMARINE
youth and health.

APRIL – DIAMOND
eternity and courage.

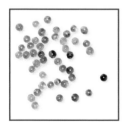

MAY – EMERALD
happiness and fertility.

JUNE – PEARL
purity and innocence.

JULY – RUBY
peace and harmony.

AUGUST – PERIDOT
dignity and morality.

SEPTEMBER – SAPPHIRE
wisdom and mercy.

OCTOBER – OPAL
love and hope.

NOVEMBER –TOPAZ
providence and good luck.

DECEMBER – TURQUOISE
prosperity and piety.

SOURCES OF INSPIRATION

Ideas for using colour are all around us. There are stunning colour combinations found in nature – gardening, animal or landscape books are a good resource – or look for effective colour schemes around the home, such as a favourite garment, a pretty postcard, a funky tablemat or some gorgeous wrapping paper. Keep some tear sheets of your favourite magazine images that you can use later for inspiration.

Blue is universally recognised as the colour of the sea and sky; a natural colour with a calming effect that is believed to bring peace and is the colour of mourning in some cultures.

White is seen as purity, cleanliness and innocence and jewellery in subtle shades, like ivory and antique white, are chosen for bridal ceremonies in most Western countries.

Look at the inspiration source and select beads in the same colours, remembering that you will only achieve the same overall effect if you get the proportions right. The spray of orchids in the postcard (inset) inspired this pretty necklace. At first glance it appears to be mainly red and green but it has subtle touches of orange and gold that work well with the brass wire to create a triadic colour scheme. For step-by-step instructions on making the *Juicy Pearl Necklace*, see the Projects chapter.

Planning your own Jewellery

It is quite easy to string an interesting selection of beads together for a simple necklace or a pretty bracelet but as you strive to create more complicated designs and to make other types of jewellery such as rings, earrings, brooches and even a tiara or two, the question will arise: what makes a well-designed piece of jewellery?

DESIGN CONCEPTS

Successful jewellery design depends on putting elements together in an attractive way so that it appears so perfectly balanced and complete that nothing added or taken away would improve it. Even the simplest piece of jewellery has several design concepts at play – proportion, movement and harmony. In more complex pieces of jewellery, contrast, dominance and repetition are brought into the mix.

HARMONY uses different elements to produce an overall pleasing effect.
• Too much similarity can make a design boring and dull.
• Add dynamism with small contrasts in colour, shape, size and texture.
• Avoid too many visual differences, which confuse the eye.

CONTRAST adds dynamism and energy to a design.
• Beads all the same can be monotonous but too much contrast can be overwhelming.
• Use slight contrasts in texture, tone or size to create a more interesting piece.
• Experiment with different shapes, colours and materials to create dynamic designs.

MOVEMENT AND RHYTHM gives life to your creations.
• It refers to the physical movement as well as the way different elements work together.
• Create movement by varying shapes and lines.
• Add rhythm with skilful use of pattern, grading bead colours and sizes.

*Using contrasting shapes and sizes in pretty pastel beads creates an exciting but **harmonious** design.*

*Repetition of pattern and beads gives a sense of **rhythm** while the graded colours and tassel strands create **movement**.*

*Adding contrast with the shiny cubes and golden yellow beads makes this design more **dynamic**.*

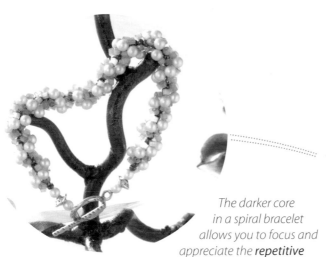

The darker core in a spiral bracelet allows you to focus and appreciate the **repetitive** spirals of pale pearls.

Using purple as a **dominant colour** holds the different elements of these earrings together.

REPETITION brings cohesiveness to the design.
• Repeat elements like groups of beads, colour or patterns.
• Balance the repetition with a focal point to draw the eye in.
• Use brighter or darker colours, a larger bead or pendant to create a focal point.

DOMINANCE pulls all the elements of a piece of jewellery together.
• Dominance in colour or composition gives jewellery a sense of unity.
• Increasing an element, such as colour, texture or shape creates a more coherent design.
• Create a more exciting design by increasing other elements rather than colour.

PROPORTION is the key to good design.
• Proportion refers to the relationship of component parts of jewellery and the design as a whole.
• Balance the size of individual elements such as beads and findings.
• Arrange elements carefully so that they are pleasing to the eye.

SIZE alters the look of jewellery considerably.
• The size of the components influences the design of all pieces of jewellery.
• Consider using large blocks of colour for impact.
• Elements such as chain, ribbon or cord can make a piece delicate or chunky.

WEIGHT helps jewellery to hang well and creates movement.
• Heavy components and beads can make earrings and necklaces uncomfortable to wear.
• Distribution of weight is crucial in allowing a necklace or pendant to hang correctly.
• Too much weight can create a lopsided effect or cause a bracelet to swing round to the underside.

Chunky findings balance the **weight and size** of these beads, which graduate down towards the focal heart charm.

A large, square pendant needs sufficient strands of seed beads to create the bulk for a balanced, **chunky effect**.

Designing a Necklace

There are lots of different ways to design a necklace: you can begin with an image of one you like, a colour scheme, or perhaps you need something for a particular occasion. If you start with single strand necklaces, learning how to compose the design and choose the beads, it will be easy to progress to more complicated designs using some of the concepts discussed in the section on planning your own jewellery.

PLANNING THE DESIGN

When making a necklace, first decide if you want to have a focal point, such as a large bead or a cluster of beads and, if so, where to have it. This is usually in the centre, either strung on the bead string or hanging below as a pendant. A focal point at one side is known as a station. Flat beads or embellishments work best in this position and can be extremely flattering close to the collarbone.

CHOOSE YOUR STYLE

Single strand beaded necklaces fall into three main styles. There is the formal style where both sides of the design are of equal weight, which includes the classic pearl necklace with graduated beads. Necklaces with an informal balance have larger beads on one side of the necklace than the other and mosaic necklaces look like the beads have been chosen randomly from a bead mix. Although it sounds simple, this necklace is sometimes the trickiest to design.

*This multistrand seed bead necklace is all the more stunning because it has a long bone bead as a **station** or focal point at one side.*

*Add interest to a simple necklace by using a much larger bead as a **station** in the centre. In this macramé necklace the beads are from the same range and look stunning.*

*Pendant beads draw the eye and form the focal point at the bottom of a necklace creating a more interesting **Y-shaped** design.*

GRADE YOUR BEADS

Following colour theory (see Creating with Colour, arrange your beads in terms of primary (the main focus of the necklace or bracelet and usually the most expensive), secondary (for framing and enhancing the primary beads) and tertiary (for filling the gaps in between, usually the least expensive) elements. Lay the beads out on a bead mat or, better still, use a bead board (see Other Equipment) as you can build up the design knowing that it is going to be the right length.

NECKLACE LENGTHS

Weight is important when making a necklace. If it is long and heavy it can be uncomfortable to wear, but if beads, particularly pendants, are too light, the necklace may not lie properly when worn. These are standard lengths of necklace but take into account the height of the person and their body shape when planning the design and adjust if necessary. Necklaces longer than 61cm (24in) don't need a fastening.

Choker: 36–41cm (14–16in)
Pendant: 46cm (18in)
Matinee: 51–61cm (20–24in)
Opera: 71–81cm (28–32in)
Rope: 101–114cm (40–45in)
Lariat: over 114cm (45in)

*A **choker** is the shortest length of necklace.*

*A classic pearl string has a formal style in **matinee** length.*

*A **lariat** is a long, open-ended necklace that can be worn in lots of different ways.*

Materials and Tools

Materials and equipment for jewellery making are readily available from craft and bead shops or online. Before beginning to make beaded jewellery you will need some stringing material and some basic tools and you can then add specialist items as specific projects require them.

Stringing Material

There are dozens of threads, cords and ribbons as well as traditional bead stringing materials that can be used for jewellery making. This selection provides an overview of what's available to help you choose the most suitable, depending on the technique you plan to use and the look you're after.

THICKER MATERIALS

LEATHER THONG is a round shiny cord traditionally used for hanging pendants.
- It is useful for stringing beads with large holes.
- Simply knot the ends as it doesn't fray.
- Available in a range of thicknesses.

SOFT SUEDE is a flat matt strip with the characteristic rough texture of suede.
- It can be natural, but is more likely to be faux suede.
- Available in a wide range of colours, both bold and pastel.
- Usually about 2.5 or 3mm thick (about ⅛in).

WAX COTTON is a round cord that looks fabulous in knotted designs.
- Useful for stringing beads with large holes and works well with ribbon.
- Refresh the cord by pressing with a hot iron.
- Generally available in 1–2mm (about ¹⁄₁₆in) thickness.

SATIN CORD is a silky polyester cord.
- Use it for pendants and knotted designs or twist to make silky ropes.
- Available in 2mm (rattail), 1.5mm (mousetail) and 1mm (bugtail).
- Delicate surface that can become damaged from overuse.

YARNS are usually sold for knitting.
- Decorative synthetic fibres especially attractive in jewellery.
- Use natural yarns like linen or jute instead of cord or string for macramé.
- Weave through a chunky chain to add texture.

*Because **multifilament threads** are available in a wide range of colours that can be matched exactly to the beads, they are ideal for bead stringing.*

THREAD FOR BEAD STITCHING

MULTIFILAMENTS are strong, flat threads, generally pre-waxed and lightly twisted.
- Tangle-resistant and colourfast .
- Can be tied in a tight knot.
- Each make has slightly different properties; Nymo™, KO™ and Superlon™ are popular.

BRAIDED THREADS are multiple strand threads that have been plaited (braided) together.
- A very strong thread that doesn't stretch.
- Good for stitching or stringing beads with sharp edges such as bugles and crystals.
- Makes include Dandyline™, Fireline™ and PowerPro™. A 4–6lb weight is appropriate for bead stitching.

STRINGING THREADS AND WIRE

BEAD CORD is used for jewellery where you want the thread to be visible.
- Unwaxed bead cord is attractive and supple, for good drape and movement.
- Choose silk cord with an inbuilt needle for knotting pearls.
- Stiffer synthetic cord threads are available with or without wax in a range of thicknesses.

MONOFILAMENTS are threads with a single strand.
- Elastic, illusion cord and fishing line are all monofilaments.
- Floating (illusion) necklaces are made from clear monofilament threads.
- Elastic cords stretch to fit and don't require fastenings; hide the knot in a bead.

BEAD STRINGING WIRE is composed of fine wires coated with nylon thread.
- Select by the number of strands first (49, 19 or 7 strands) and then by diameter.
- Match the bead hole size and weight to diameter; 0.018in is a good standard size.
- 49 strands gives better drape and flexibility, 7 strands is inexpensive and 19 strands a good all-rounder.

THREAD THICKNESS

The thickness of the thread should be matched to the size of the bead holes to avoid loose beads rubbing and causing the thread to fray and snap. In general, a double strand of a thinner thread is more secure than one thicker thread. Thread sizes vary depending on the make, with either a letter or number indicating the size. Letter sizes, from finest to thickest, are 00, A, B, C, D, E, F, FF, G. D is ideal for bead stitching with seed beads, E or F for medium weight beads and F or G for heavy beads. Weight strengths are given for threads that were originally fishing line, such as Fireline, Grandslam and Power Pro, and range from 4–80lb (0.06–0.46mm). A 4lb line is equivalent to size B and 6lb line to size D.

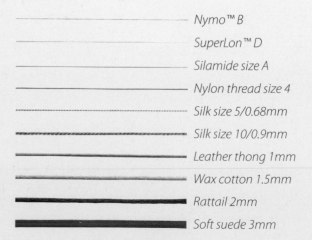

Nymo™ B
SuperLon™ D
Silamide size A
Nylon thread size 4
Silk size 5/0.68mm
Silk size 10/0.9mm
Leather thong 1mm
Wax cotton 1.5mm
Rattail 2mm
Soft suede 3mm

Wire and Chain

Wire and chain are versatile materials that allow a great degree of freedom to form shapes and create structure in your designs. Wirework is the term used to describe making wire jewellery and components. You will need a basic set of jewellery tools (see the Equipment section) to work with chain and wire.

WIRE

There are all sorts of wires available for jewellery making ranging from cheap craft wire to sterling silver and even gold. The guide below will give you an idea of what is suitable for different types of jewellery.

PLATED WIRES with a copper core are economical substitutes for silver and gold.
• Avoid poor quality wire as the plating will wear off in use.
• Not suitable for shaping with a hammer as it is too soft and the copper core shows through if damaged.
• A good standard size for wire wrapping and earring links is 0.6mm (24 swg).

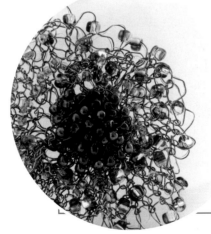

ENAMELLED WIRES are available in a wide range of colours and thicknesses.
• They make exciting designs when matched to the bead colours.
• The enamelling can be damaged easily.
• Use pliers with nylon jaws or fine serrations on the flat surfaces to work.

PRECIOUS METAL WIRES, such as sterling silver and gold-filled, are expensive options for everyday jewellery.
• Available in a range of thicknesses and hardness: soft, half-hard and hard are the most common.
• Use with a chasing hammer to make your own fastenings and findings.
• Different cross sections such as square, rectangular and D-shaped are also available.

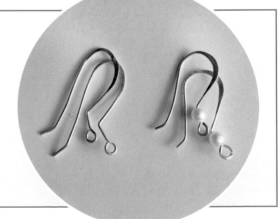

BASE METALS are technically metals like copper that corrode or oxidise easily.
• Now the term encompasses all metals, other than precious-metal, including bronze, brass and aluminium.
• Some of these inexpensive metals can give jewellery an antique appearance.
• Aluminium wire is available in a range of bright colours, generally over 1mm (19swg). It is very soft and can be easily shaped by hand.

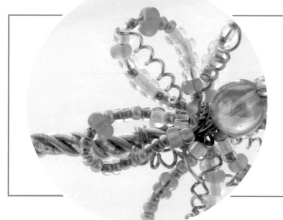

COATED WIRES are covered in paper, thread or plastic.
• They add a contemporary look to jewellery.
• Available in a range of thicknesses and colours.
• Avoid using paper for items that will get wet.

MEMORY WIRE is an extremely hard wire available in different sized coils.
• Holds its circular shape in sizes for rings, bracelets and necklaces.
• Should be cut with heavyweight or special memory wire cutters only.
• The coils open out to accommodate different sizes of beads.

To finish the end of memory wire, either apply a drop of instant glue to the tip of the wire and insert into a ball end, or bend the wire over.

When working with wire or chain, especially precious metals, save any scraps as they can be recycled.

WIRE GAUGES

Wires are available in a range of thicknesses or gauges – sold in millimetres, standard wire gauge (swg) or American wire gauge (awg). The thinnest wire that will hold its shape as a bead link or plain loop is 0.6mm (24 swg), which has a lovely delicate appearance. More secure is 0.8mm (21swg), but it gives a slightly chunkier look. For wrapping and knitting or crochet, 0.2mm (36swg) and 0.315mm (30swg) are good.

mm	swg	awg
0.1	42	38
0.15	38	34
0.2	36	32
0.25	33	30
0.315	30	28
0.4	27	26
0.5	25	24
0.6	24	22
0.7	22	21
0.8	21	20
0.9	20	19
1.0	19	18
1.2	18	16
1.5	16	14
2.0	14	12

WIRE TEMPER

Wire, in particular sterling silver wire, is sold in different levels of hardness, which is a measure of the ease that the wire will bend. You will need to experiment to find what is suitable for the task in hand.

SOFT WIRE is useful for wrapping around another wire or for crochet and knitting.
- It is less likely to snap or break as you work it.
- It doesn't hold its shape well and easily marked with tools or a hammer.
- Simple components can be tempered (hardened) by hitting with a hammer (see Hammering Wire).

HALF-HARD is a good, versatile all-round wire.
- Easy to manipulate to make coils and sharp angles and holds its shape fairly well.
- Suitable for jump rings, clasps and connectors.
- Harden the component with a hammer so it holds its shape.

HARD WIRE is the least flexible wire.
- You need tools to bend it but it makes good sharp corners.
- It doesn't require further hardening to hold its shape.
- It becomes progressively more difficult to manipulate the more it is worked.

CHAIN

Chain has become one of the most popular elements in jewellery design and the variety available is now phenomenal. Choose chain to complement the beads so that the design works as a whole.

BASE METAL chains are made from copper, brass and bronze. They can also be plated with a wide range of colours.
• Can be used to give jewellery an antique appearance.
• Various patinas are available to replicate this antique appearance on plain metal findings and wire.
• Available in a wide range of link sizes and shapes.

PRECIOUS METAL chains include fine silver, sterling silver, bali silver, gold and rolled gold.
• Usually have soldered links for security because the metal is more expensive.
• Sold by the foot (30cm).
• Can be extremely fine and add a sense of quality to jewellery designs.

POLYESTER CHAIN is a new style of nylon-coated plastic chain.
• Quite chunky but very lightweight.
• Has solid rings and so quite secure and strong.
• Available in black and a range of colours, usually in 1m (1yd) lengths.

Chain is available in a range of metals, metallic finishes and colours.

Equipment

There is a range of tools available to help you get the best results when making jewellery. The basic tool kit of flat-nose pliers, round-nose pliers and wire cutters is all you need to begin – you can invest in more specialist tools and equipment as required. Choose relatively fine tools, as you will usually be working on a small scale.

1 FLAT-NOSE PLIERS

These have flat jaws with a slightly rough surface to grip wire or findings. Some are called snipe- or chain-nose pliers, which taper towards the tip, and others have a blunt end (blunt-nose). Bent-nose pliers are a variation of snipe-nose that allow you to get into confined areas (1a).

2 ROUND-NOSE PLIERS

Used for making plain loops, jump rings and for springs or coiling. The conical shaped jaws are tapered to make a range of loop sizes. Work near the tip for tiny loops and the base of the jaws for larger rings. Three-step round-nose pliers are perfect for making the same size of loop again and again (2a).

3 WIRE CUTTERS

Known as side or end cutters depending on the position of the cutting jaws, these are essential for cutting and trimming wire. Small cutters with fine tips allow you to get closer to the work. End cutters are stronger and more suitable for cutting thicker wire (3a). Choose top quality flush cutters for making jump rings as they trim the wire with a completely flat end (3b).

4 NYLON JAW PLIERS

Available as either round- or flat-nose, these are specialist tools used for straightening wire and for working with very soft wires such as aluminium and dead soft sterling silver.

5 CRIMPING PLIERS

Used to secure crimps and crimp tubes and produce a more professional finish than flat-nose pliers. Available in several sizes to suit different sizes of crimp, they put a dent in one side and then you squeeze the bent crimp to make a neat rounded shape.

6 SPLIT RING PLIERS

Indispensable if you use split rings on a regular basis. The special tip is designed to open the ring so that you can attach a finding.

1

2

3

4

1a

2a

3a

3b

5

6

WAX AND CONDITIONER

Used to coat thread for bead stitching, prevents tangling and helps to keep the beadwork tight as you stitch. Products such as Thread Heaven and microcrystalline wax are available. Remove excess by running the thread between your finger and thumb before you begin.

THREAD ZAPPER

Makes it easy to cut thread close to bead stitching. Natural or man-made thread burns and synthetic threads melt and so there are no unsightly, tiny ends sticky out between the beads.

BEAD STOPPER SPRINGS

Indispensable as a bead stop when bead stitching or generally to prevent beads falling off a bead string. There are several sizes available, but small springs are easier to work around.

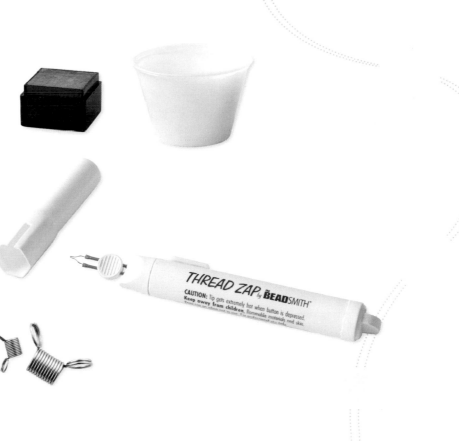

NEEDLES

There are a wide variety of needles suitable for different types of beadwork. Beading needles can be very fine and are easily bent so do keep them in a box or needle case when not in use.

1 TAPESTRY NEEDLES

These have a relatively blunt tip and are useful for stringing large beads onto cord or ribbon. They are also used to manoeuvre knots into position.

2 BIG EYE NEEDLES

These have a long eye that stretches the length of the needle and are ideal for threading beads onto ribbon or yarn.

3 TWISTED WIRE NEEDLES

Available in several sizes, or you can make your own. They are used for threading through beads with tiny holes. The round eye is easy to thread, but collapses as it is pulled through the beads.

4 CURVED BIG EYE NEEDLES

Specialist needles for stringing beads directly from a bead spinner. The curved tip is dipped into the beads and allows the beads to flow onto the needle.

5 SEWING NEEDLES

Use in similar sizes to beading needles for beadwork. Sharps have small round eyes and are suitable for bead stitching and embroidery. Crewel or embroidery needles have longer eyes for thicker threads and large-holed beads.

6 BEADING NEEDLES

Finie needles with a flat eye, which goes through tiny bead holes easily. A size 10 or 12 needle is suitable for regular seed beads, but you will need a size 13 needle for the tiny size 15 seed beads or if you need to take thread through regular seed beads several times.

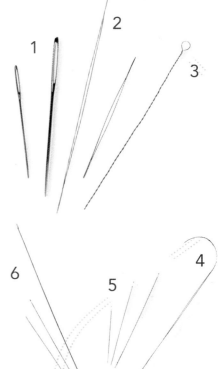

Other Equipment

As your interest in making jewellery grows you'll begin to look for ways to get a more professional finish. The tools and equipment on these next few pages include some tools for specific techniques and others that just make it easier to make jewellery.

BEAD MAT

Made from a fine microfibre, these are inexpensive and almost indispensable. The short pile stops beads rolling about and helps you pick up directly onto the needle. When finished, it is easy to fold the mat and tip unused beads back into the container.

BEAD SCOOPS AND TRAYS

Available in a range of shapes and sizes, they are useful for picking up beads and putting them back into containers.

NECKLACE PLANNING BOARD

Useful aid when stringing beads for necklaces and bracelets. The grooves hold the beads in position and the curved shape gives a good impression of the finished result. The board also has measurements marked to help plan the design.

MANDRELS

Tubes or rods that you wrap wire round to create particular shapes or use to support tubular bead stitching. You can buy special tools that are graded to make a range of ring sizes or to create different shapes, but knitting needles, crochet hooks and bead tubes are equally useful.

CALIPER

A clever tool for measuring the size of beads. You can usually measure in both inches or millimetres on the same tool.

EZ-SIZER

Cone-shaped mandrel with graded measurements marked to allow you to make bracelets and necklaces the right size. Wrap the jewellery around the tool at the correct height and adjust the number of beads, allowing room for a fastening.

RING MANDREL

Used in tandem with a ring sizer to make rings the correct size. Use the sizer to find out what size of ring you need and then use the mandrel to create the ring the right size.

CUP BUR

Useful for rounding off ends of wire, especially when making your own earring wires and fastenings.

BEAD REAMER

This has several heads, encrusted with fine diamond powder, so that you can open out bead holes or remove jagged edges that might otherwise damage the bead stringing material. For best results, dip the tip in water before using it.

FILES Used to smooth rough edges on wire or metal as well as precious metal clay. Needle files are available in a range of shapes; use a flat needle file to smooth wire ends after trimming.

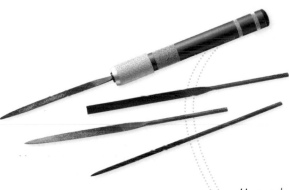

HAMMERS

Used in jewellery making to shape, texture and harden wire and metal. A chasing hammer has a smooth metal face, which is slightly rounded, making it easy to hammer at a slight angle to taper wire. A nylon head hammer is used to straighten wire or harden it by gentle tapping.

BENCH BLOCK

A smooth hardened steel block used as a surface for hammering wire. Place on a rubber mat to deaden the noise a little and stop the block from moving around. Rubber bench blocks are also useful for straightening wire and working with precious metal clay.

WIRE JIG

Used to shape wire. It has a flat base covered in holes and pegs of different sizes to fit in the holes. The pegs are arranged then the wire wrapped round to make jewellery components and fastenings. The jig allows you to make several pieces exactly the same. A metal jig is sturdier than plastic.

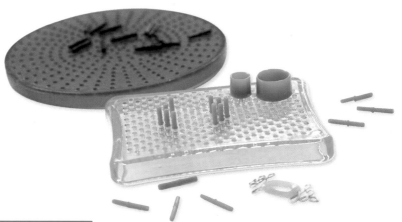

HAND DRILL AND CORDMAKERS

Used to twist wire and make cords from rattail and other materials. These tools allow you to make an even twist for a more professional finish.

KNOTTING AWL

Used to manoeuvre the knots between beads. It has a long tapered point and a handle for ease of use; a paper pricker or even a tapestry needle, is a suitable alternative. A knotting tool is a professional tool for knotting between beads and useful if you plan to make lots of pearl necklaces.

STRAND HOLDER

Any piece of equipment that you can use to hold multiple threads or temporarily secure strands when making some necklaces and tassels. Use anything that can be opened and closed easily such as a knitting stitch holder, a carabiner or even a metal shower ring. Bead stopper springs are useful for holding several fine strings.

STORAGE CONTAINERS

Hobby boxes with secure lids are available in a range of styles and sizes. Workboxes available from hardware stores are useful for wires and tools but beads need to be secured in lidded containers or ziplock bags. Items like sweet boxes with flip-top lids, film canisters and food containers can be used to store a range of beading equipment.

GLUES

There are several types of glue used for jewellery making. Remember to work in a well-ventilated area and take particular care when using instant bond glue as it sticks to skin.

EPOXY RESIN

A very strong, two-part glue used to secure brooch backs or to stick components together. Look for quick setting glue that dries clear for jewellery making.

JEWELLERY GLUE

Clear glue that takes a little while to dry but remains flexible when it sets. It is generally used for securing knots. Popular makes include E6000 and G-S Hypo Cement that has a very fine nozzle for precision application.

INSTANT BOND

Also called superglue, it sets very quickly but dries hard and may become brittle and break. Available in a gel form, which is less likely to leach along bead thread or illusion cord when securing beads.

A cocktail stick or toothpick is useful for applying tiny amounts of glue.

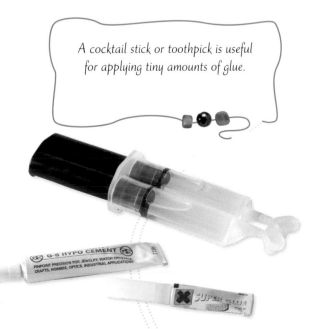

Findings

Findings are all the little pieces, generally made of metal, that are used to make and finish items of jewellery. Listed in this chapter are the basic findings you will need, as well as decorative findings which, whilst not essential, can be used to create some stunning designs.

Basics

These are the workhorses of the findings range and it is important to keep a small supply of all these pieces so that you can create different styles of jewellery. Essential items include jump rings, headpins and calottes.

JUMP RINGS
Round or oval; used to connect sections of jewellery or to attach findings; open and close with pliers but the resulting tiny gap makes them insecure for heavier beads.

Keep a wide selection of findings in your beading kit so you are free to change a design and to inspire you to be creative.

SPLIT RINGS
Made from a coil (like a keyring) so more secure than jump rings; ideal for attaching fastenings securely; can be opened by hand but easier with a pair of split ring pliers.

HEADPINS
Straight wire findings of different lengths and thicknesses; have a flat or decorative end to stop beads falling off; use to make bead dangles with one or more beads (see the Plain Loop technique).

EYEPINS
Straight pieces of wire of different lengths with a loop at one end; for joining jewellery elements; use to create bead links, with a loop at both ends, or for decorative bead dangles by coiling or bending the tail of the wire.

Crimp ends like E-Z crimps have a built-in coil that grips bead stringing wire when squeezed. Insert the bead stringing wire into the finding and then use crimp pliers to secure. Tug the wire to check it isn't loose.

CRIMPS
Tiny donut or tubular shaped metal pieces used in place of a knot to make loops, attach findings or space beads; secure with flat-nose or crimp pliers.

CALOTTES (OR BEAD TIPS)

Little, domed findings used to neatly secure thread ends or bead stringing wire; choose from basic calottes or more secure clamshell calottes.

CORD ENDS

Used to finish cord, ribbon, thong or rattail neatly; attach ring to fastenings and fold over metal lugs with pliers to secure the length(s) of stringing material.

SPRING ENDS

A type of cord end; a tight spring, made from a hard wire, with one ring bent for attaching fastenings to; threading material is inserted in the other end and flat- or snipe-nose pliers used to squeeze the end of the spring to secure.

CRIMP ENDS

Generally used with bead stringing wire; designed for either single or multiple strands; insert stringing material and flatten tubular crimp ends with flat-nose pliers; for styles with a soft metal tube in the middle, secure with snipe-nose pliers.

END CONES

Used to cover raw edges of thicker cords and ribbons ready to attach fastenings; most have a hole at the top so stringing material can be secured with wire or an eyepin; choose a shape and size for a close fit.

Ribbon clamps (or end bars) are similar to end cones in that they are designed to cover the raw ends of ribbon, but they can be used to finish macramé or plaited necklaces too. Apply a narrow strip of adhesive tape to hold the yarns temporarily until the teeth along each edge of the clamp grip the fibres.

Finishing

These findings are essential too as they are used to fasten or attach the jewellery. You will not need all of these at once but a selection of styles of fastening, a brooch back or two, and a few different earring findings will let you experiment and be inspired to create a new design.

TOGGLE FASTENING
Two-part fastening consisting of T-bar and hoop or ring; turn T-bar on its side to slot in or out of the hoop; many styles available; can be used as a design feature in a necklace or bracelet.

TRIGGER CLASP
Range of shapes and sizes available including basic bolt ring, and lobster clasp with pinching mechanism; all have spring-loaded trigger for opening; suitable for both bracelets and necklaces.

SCREW FASTENING
Barrel-shaped; also known as torpedo or barrel fastening; has two similar-shaped ends that screw together; suitable for lightweight necklaces only; unsuitable for bracelets as impossible to close with one hand.

MAGNETIC FASTENING
Secured with a strong magnet; basic barrel-shaped magnetic fastenings for lightweight necklaces and bracelets; more ornate multi-strand fastenings for heavier cuff-style bracelets.

MULTI-STRAND CLASPS
Available in a range of shapes and sizes for stringing multiple strands; box clasps style suitable for necklaces; slider clasps ideal for bracelets.

Box clasps are available for single or multi-strands and can be quite large and decorative or tiny like the one used here.

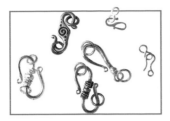

S-HOOK FASTENING

Ideal for necklaces but unsuitable for bracelets as comes undone too easily; can be double-ended, looking exactly like an 'S', or have a hook at one end and a ring at the other.

CRIMP FASTENING

For neatly securing bead stringing wire or illusion cord; use tubular crimp fastenings to neatly secure multiple strands.

RING BASES

Available in a wide range of styles and metal finishes; either attach beads directly to the rings with headpins, sew the beads onto a mesh or attach with epoxy resin.

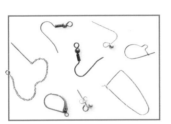

EARRING WIRES

Designed for pierced ears; shapes include kidney, fish hook, posts and hoops; available in a range of metal finishes; the more expensive, sterling silver wires are least likely to produce an allergic reaction.

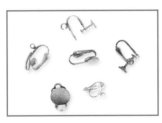

EARRING FITMENTS

Clip- or screw-on earring fitments for unpierced ears; varied styles available; slightly bulkier than earring wires; may have a small ring for attaching a bead motif or cabochon.

*These **rings with a clasp opening** are used to shorten strings of beads or can be used as a fastening for chain or bead stitched rope bracelets and necklaces.*

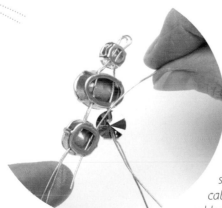

***Settings** are used to secure no-hole beads such as fancy stones and cabochons. They can be soldered or wired together.*

Design Details

Introducing different metal elements as design details can make your beaded jewellery more innovative. As well as a range of findings, there are also specially designed items that can be used to make attractive jewellery and accessories.

BEAD CAP

Cup-shaped components that sit on one or both sides of a bead to adorn it; choose a size that fits snugly over the bead; can be plain or elaborate in different metal finishes.

CONNECTORS

Used to join elements in jewellery, they have two holes or rings and can be functional or quite decorative.

CHANDELIERS

Wire or moulded findings used to create different styles of earrings or pendants when additional beads or elements are added to the loops.

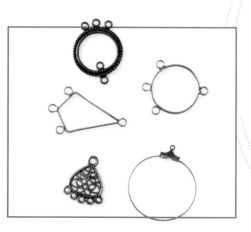

SPACER BARS

Long, thin strips, or more substantial decorative bars, with holes along the length; use to hold strings of beads side by side; finish the jewellery with matching bar ends.

BAR ENDS

Decorative bars with holes along the length and a loop to attach a fastening; used for multistrand necklaces and bracelets; can be used with spacer bars.

STAMPINGS OR FILIGREE FINDINGS

Intricate pierced metal components that can be used as a design element in jewellery or embellished with beads; some have holes for hanging.

SOLID RINGS

Different shaped rings used as a connector or focal element in jewellery design; attach to beads, chain or string material with jump rings or wrapped loops.

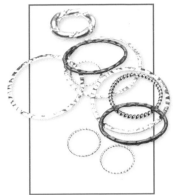

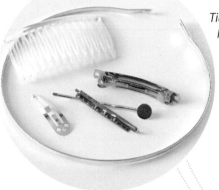

Tiara bands, hair combs, barrettes and hair clips, available in different metal finishes, are just some of the items you can embellish with beads.

Everyday items like watch faces, key rings, kilt pins and mobile phone charms are available from bead shops, designed specially to be embellished. You can use different techniques from wirework to bead stitching.

*Fancy stones from the SWAROVSKI ELEMENTS range of beads don't have holes but each style has its own specific setting. These settings can be soldered together or, as they have holes in the side, can be sewn together with fine wire to create a cluster of beads that is then attached to a brooch or ring base with strong glue. Arrange the settings as shown or choose your own arrangement to create a unique design. For step-by-step instructions to make the **Crystal Statement Ring**, see the Projects chapter.*

Stringing

String an interesting selection of beads together and you've made a simple necklace or bracelet. However, learning a little about stringing material, different techniques and ways of finishing may create a better design. This chapter covers everything you need to know to string beads on any type of thread or cord.

Choosing Threads

The sheer variety of threads and cords can be overwhelming so to help make a selection, the most popular threads are listed below with guidance about which to use where. The weight of the beads and size of the hole determines the strength and thickness of the stringing material required (see Thread Thickness).

Material	General advice	Uses	Finishing method
Bead stringing wire	Choose the correct flexibility (number of strands) for your design – 49 strands is the most flexible, then 19 and 7. Use crimps to space beads and attach fastenings.	Floating necklaces; stringing beads for a firm, curved shape; heavy or sharp-edged beads; designs where the stringing material is the main focus.	Crimp beads and tubes; crimp ends; crimp fastenings; calottes with crimps then regular fastenings.
Silk cord	Usually has an inbuilt needle to thread through smaller holes. Will fray against sharp edged beads and findings; attractive colours to use as a design feature.	Stringing smooth edged beads like pearls; spacing beads with knots; thicker threads can be used with chunky beads.	Gimp; wire guardians; calottes; regular fastenings.
Braided threads	Basic colours as designed to be hidden by beads; strong thread that doesn't stretch; can be knotted or secure thicker threads with crimps.	Good for stringing beads with sharp edges; use to string longer necklace styles.	Calottes; gimp; wire guardians; regular fastenings.
Monofilaments	Use thick thread for the main string and fine thread to hang beads for illusion effect; secure beads with glue or knots.	Illusion necklaces; children's or casual necklaces with medium to heavyweight beads.	Calottes and regular fastenings; crimp fastenings.
Satin cord	Easily damaged so best for special occasion jewellery; available in several thicknesses, (for example rattail, mousetail etc.) and colours.	Pendants; beads with large holes; use for top section of necklace; make into a rope as a design feature.	Thong, spring, crimp ends or end caps with regular fastening; large diameter crimp fastenings.

Waxed cotton, hemp, linen etc.	Limited lifespan; inexpensive; need no special tools; suitable for ethnic and casual styles; wax cotton available in bright and pastel shades, others usually natural colours.	Knotted necklaces and bracelets including macramé; pendants; multiple strands as a design feature.	Slip and slide fastenings, thong, spring, crimp ends or end caps with regular fastenings; crimp fastenings.
Leather thong and (faux) suede	Attractive so can be a feature; doesn't fray; good for large hole beads.	Pendants; casual necklaces; knotted jewellery.	As waxed cotton (see above).
Elastic thread	Suitable for children as size of wearer not crucial; beads should sit together but must stretch enough to come off.	Casual bracelets and necklaces.	Knot or crimp ends together and hide inside a large hole bead.
Memory wire	Use heavyweight cutters only; size expands to fit wearer.	Rings, bracelets and necklaces; cut into a single loop or use multiple coils.	Finish ends by bending over with pliers or glue ball ends in place.

Finishing Without a Fastening

Necklaces that are over 60cm (24in) in length, as well as shorter necklaces or bracelets strung with elastic, don't need a fastening. Choose from the following techniques.

ELASTIC THREAD

1. Tie the ends together, working two reef knots one after the other (see Tying Knots). Trim the ends and hide the knot inside one of the beads with a larger hole.

2. Alternatively, feed the opposite ends through a crimp and squeeze with flat-nose pliers or crimp pliers to secure. Two crimps placed a few beads apart is even more secure. Pass end through a few beads before trimming. Bead stringing wire can be joined with crimps in the same way as elastic.

BEAD THREAD OR CORD

1. You can simply tie the ends together using a reef knot but this is a more secure technique. String the beads, leaving 10cm (4in) at each end. Pass one end of the string through several beads.

2. Using the tail thread, work a half-hitch knot (see Tying Knots) over the main thread. Pass the end through another two beads and knot again. Secure each knot with a drop of jewellery glue. Repeat with the other tail, in the opposite direction. Pass the ends through a few more beads and trim the ends.

Adding Fastenings

Most necklace designs require a fastening and you will usually need to cover the thread ends before attaching it. The method you choose usually depends on the stringing material used – refer to the Thread Guide.

CLAMSHELL CALOTTE

Clamshell calottes are knot covers that provide a neat way to finish the thread ends securely. They have a hole within the hinge at the bottom.

1. Feed the clamshell calotte onto the bead string so that the open side is nearest the tail. Tie a figure of eight or two overhand knots (see Tying Knots). Trim the end close to the knot.

2. Add a tiny drop of jewellery glue to the knot. Slide the clamshell calotte down so that the knot is inside, then close the two sides of the calotte with flat-nosed pliers.

3. String your beads and thread a clamshell calotte on the other end. Tie an overhand knot. Use a tapestry needle or beading awl to slide the knot inside the calotte. If necessary tie a second overhand knot.

4. Fold the metal loop on one calotte over a jump ring and flatten with snipe-nosed pliers to secure. Attach a second jump ring to the clasp and secure the second calotte in the same way.

CALOTTE

This has the same purpose as a clamshell calotte but has a hinge at the side and a hole at the bottom.

1. Tie a figure of eight or overhand knot on the end of the bead string. Trim the end and apply a drop of glue. Lay the knot inside the calotte so that the bead string is in the groove at the bottom and close the two sides with flat-nosed pliers.

2. String the beads and tie a knot at the other end. Attach a second calotte over the knot. Open a jump ring and attach to the loop on the calotte, then attach a jump ring and fastening to the other end.

USING GIMP

Gimp, or French bullion, is a tight spiral of fine wire that is used to protect bead string, especially silk cord, from fraying against findings. The gimp covers the short section of thread that goes through the fastening.

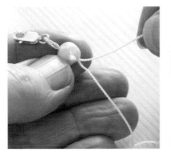   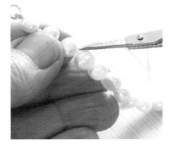

1. Pick up three beads; push down to the end of the bead cord. Tie a loose knot on the end. Cut a 12mm (½in) length of gimp with flush cutters and thread onto the cord. Pick up a fastening, take the needle back through the first bead again and pull up to make a loop with the gimp, leaving the tail with the three pearls on it at least 8cm (3in) long.

2. Tie a half-hitch (see Tying Knots) after the first bead using the main beading thread. Take the needle through the next bead and make another half-hitch. Apply a drop of glue to one or both of these knots. Take the needle through the third bead. Pick up the remaining beads on the string, leaving the tail out to one side.

3. Pick up a short length of gimp and a soldered jump ring. Take the needle through the last bead. Pull up to leave a little ease between the next two beads for the knots. Tie a half-hitch between the last two beads.

4. Pass the needle through the next bead and tie a second half-hitch. Finally pass the needle through the third bead from the end. Trim both tails of cord, adding a drop of glue to each knot.

A string of pearls is one of the classic pieces of jewellery that is never out of fashion. This pretty bracelet, with fresh water pearls strung on silk cord, is knotted between each bead. Traditionally, gimp is used to protect the silk thread from fraying against the fastening. Although simple to look at, pearl knotting requires patience and a little practise to get the knots and beads sitting snugly together. See the Projects chapter for step-by-step instructions for making the **Silky Pearl Bracelet***.*

Beading Wire

Bead stringing wire, unless very fine and flexible, is not suitable for knotting and so crimps are used to attach fastenings and space beads. There are two types of crimp, a crimp bead and a crimp tube. It is essential to match the size of the crimp to the stringing material; the wire should fill as much of the crimp as possible.

Wire diameter	Crimp bead	Crimp tube	Crimp pliers
X small 0.33mm (0.013in)	0–1	1–2	Micro
Small 0.38mm (0.015in)	1	2	Regular
Medium 0.46mm (0.018in)	1	2	Regular
Large 0.6mm (0.024in)	2–3	2–3	Regular – Mighty
X large 0.76mm (0.030in)	3	4	Mighty

This chart gives some of the most popular sizes of wire with the recommended crimp size and pliers. You can also use snipe-nosed pliers with crimp beads and tubes.

USING CRIMP PLIERS

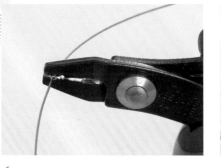

1. Position the crimp in the outer rounded groove in the crimp tool and squeeze the crimp to an oval shape.

2. Place the crimp in the inner ridged groove and squeeze so that it becomes crescent-shaped with a dip in the middle.

3. Re-position the crimp in the outer groove, so that the dip is facing sideways. Squeeze again until the crimp is rounded.

ATTACHING FASTENINGS WITH A CRIMP

Use this secure method to create a loop in bead stringing wire, monofilament or braided thread.

1. Thread the crimp on to the wire, pick up a jump ring or a fastening and feed the tail back through the crimp to create a loop. Compress the crimp (see above) so that it sits 1–2mm (1/16–1/10in) from the ring or fastening.

2. Continue stringing beads over both the tail and main wire. At the other end, pick up a crimp and a jump ring fastening. Feed the tail back through the crimp and a few beads. Compress the crimp as before and trim the tail between the beads.

HIDING CRIMPS

Crimps are not the most attractive findings to use in jewellery making. There are several ways they can be hidden when attaching fastenings, or even spacing beads.

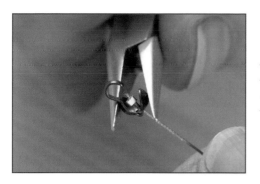

CALOTTES are generally used to cover knots but you can use them to cover crimps. Insert the beading wire through the hole in the hinge and flatten a crimp bead to secure the end of beading wire in the calotte. Close the clamshell with flat-nosed pliers.

CRIMP COVERS are crescent-shaped findings that are secured over the crimp to make a round shape. Squeeze the crimp cover gently in the (outer) rounded notch in crimping pliers until they look like very small metal beads and blend in with the jewellery design.

END CONES can be used to hide a single strand or more of bead stringing wire. Attach a fine eyepin to a crimped loop (see above) and then slide the end cone over. Trim the eyepin and make into a loop to secure a fastening.

Add a small bead if the cone hole is too big.

OTHER CRIMP FINDINGS

These findings are more secure than crimps, especially with heavier beads.

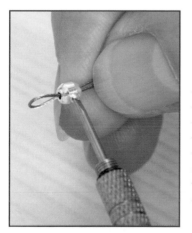

1. SCRIMPS have a tiny screw in the side that is secured with a tiny screwdriver. Loosen the screw to allow the wire to go through. Insert the wire, make a loop through a jump ring or fastening then take the wire back through the scrimp. Tighten the screw to secure, adding a tiny drop of glue.

2. CRIMP ENDS (cord ends), loop crimps and EZ crimps are designed to cover wire ends and replace crimps used with calottes. Some crimp ends and crimp fastenings have a crimp section incorporated into the design and these can be used for fine, waxed cotton and other firm threads too.

Multiple Strands

Necklaces and other jewellery with more than one strand need a little more forward planning to work out the best method of construction. The multiple strands can begin at the back of the neck or change from single to multi-strand at some other point.

MULTI-STRAND CLASPS

You can use the techniques learnt for single strand necklaces to add two or more strings, using either bead cord or bead stringing wire. Choose a clasp with enough rings for the number of strands, or use an end bar and then attach a regular clasp.

1. Attach a bead thread to each loop on the multi-strand fastening by knotting between the beads, using a calotte, or using bead stringing wire with crimps.

2. Add the beads you need on the strands, adjusting the length as required, and then attach each strand to the multi-strand fastening at the other end, making sure none are twisted.

Multi-strand necklaces can either be graduated with loops hanging one under the other or, as shown here, have the strands the same length for a fuller effect.

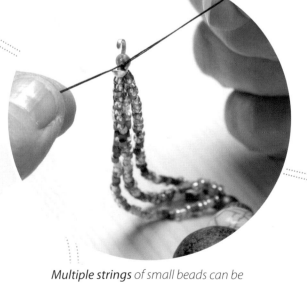

Multiple strings of small beads can be secured by knotting inside a calotte, which is then attached to a clasp.

Different styles of **bar ends** *and* **clasps** *are available to string multiple strand necklaces.*

MULTI-STRAND TO SINGLE

There are several ways to take jewellery from multi-strand to single strand. These techniques can be used with bead thread.

1. String beads onto separate threads (doubled for security) to create the multi-strand section. Thread the multiple strings onto a twisted wire or big eye needle. Thread all the strings at each end through a large accent bead and then through the remaining beads (the single strand section) of the necklace.

2. Alternatively, use an end cone to finish the multi-strands and then add beads to continue as a single strand. Add a fastening to complete.

USING END CONES

Choose an end cone that will fit snugly around the multiple strands of beads. For a neater fit, string smaller beads at the end of each strand.

1. String the beads on bead stringing wire. Make a loop on the end of each strand using a crimp. Open an eyepin and attach the loops one at a time.

2. Once all the loops are attached, close the eyepin loop. Slide the end cone onto the eyepin. Trim to 7mm (⅜in) and make into a loop with round-nosed pliers. Add a jump ring and fastening and then complete the other end in the same way.

*If you are going from multi-strand to single-strand, make a **crimp loop** on a thread of bead stringing wire and thread through the multi-strands.*

***End cones** cover several cut ends of leather thong and scrap wire, holding the chain in place in this chunky necklace.*

MULTI-STRAND SEED BEADS

Several seed bead strings can be finished with an end cone (see Using End Cones) or with a large hole bead as shown here.

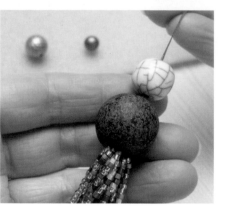

2. Thread the double thread through a bead with a large hole so that the knotted strands are hidden inside. Add the rest of the single strand of beads then attach a fastening.

1. String the multiple strands of seed beads using a bead spinner. Tie the strands together with an overhand knot (see Tying Knots), add a drop of glue and then trim the ends. Tie a double thread over the knot long enough to complete the necklace.

Use a strong, fine thread that doesn't stretch such as Fireline or another brand of braided thread to string the seed beads.

ADDING SPACER BARS

When making a multi-strand necklace or cuff-style bracelet, you can keep the strands side-by-side using spacer bars. These metal strips have two, three or more holes equally spaced along the length to correspond with a matching end bar. Plan where the bars will lie on the jewellery before beginning.

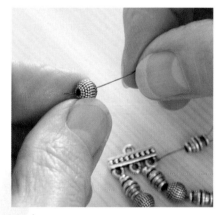

1. Attach threads or bead stringing wire to each ring on an end bar. Thread a few beads onto each strand so that each is the same length.

2. Pass one string through each hole in the spacer bar. Add more beads on each string and then add the next spacer bar. Continue to string the rest of the beads and then attach an end bar to finish.

*For **collar-style necklaces** the number of beads will increase on each strand between the bars.*

Semi-precious beads are beautiful but multi-stranded necklaces can be expensive if the beads carry round to the back of the neck. This design uses attractive, antique silver bar ends to secure the three strands and matching chain to complete the necklace and give it a contemporary look. The beautiful, green, rutile quartz briolettes, which have amazing criss-cross markings, can then be spaced for maximum impact on each strand. See the Projects chapter for step-by-step instructions for making the **Briolette Beauty**.

Spacing Beads

Those new to jewellery making begin by stringing beads side by side but one of the easiest ways to vary designs is by spacing beads. There are all sorts of reasons you may want or need to space the beads and it is useful to know some techniques for different stringing materials.

Space beads to:
- Prevent delicate beads rubbing together.
- Form a design detail.
- Link large and small beads.
- Reduce the overall weight.
- Make more expensive beads go further.

Spacer beads are usually washer-shaped and often metallic but long cylinder beads, seed beads and other small beads can be used instead.

USING SPACER BEADS

Spacer beads are one of the most useful components in jewellery making. They can be used on all types of stringing material, in particular to improve the drape or reduce the hole size in big beads so that they sit more evenly on the string.

Small round beads between large beads improve the drape, reduce the large bead hole size and reduce the overall weight of the bead string.

Rondelle spacer beads are used between the round crystals and pearls to draw in the wire mesh, to make the bead string more supple and link the large beads together.

SPACING BEADS WITH KNOTS

Bead strings are usually knotted to prevent the beads from rubbing together, to stop all of them falling off if the thread breaks, and to improve the drape of a necklace or bracelet. The traditional method is to use overhand knots, or try reef (square) knots for a more casual design. Whether you use a calotte (bead tip) or plan to string pearls with the professional gimp technique, the knots are tied and manoeuvred into position in the same way. Remember to allow an additional 3mm (⅛in) for each knot in finer threads and more for thicker threads.

OVERHAND KNOTS

This is the traditional method for knotting pearls, but can be used with other beads.
Use gimp for a more advanced professional finish.

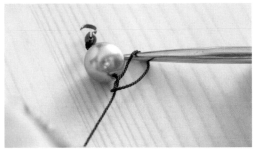

1. Attach a calotte to the end of the thread (see Calottes). Tie an overhand knot on the thread by looping the tail over and under the main thread. If you are right-handed tie with the loop to the right and if left-handed with the loop to the left. Insert a tapestry needle or beading awl into the knot and guide it up close to the calotte. Begin to pull the knot tight and remove the needle at the last moment.

2. Pick up a bead and tie another loose overhand knot. Insert the needle again and guide the loose knot along the main thread until the top of the loop sits behind the bead. This will help to keep the knot close to the bead.

> *If you use silk cord with an integral needle, you only have one strand going through each bead so the thread can be thicker and the knots larger.*

3. Gently pull the thread to slowly tighten the knot; keep the needle in the loop, bringing the tip of the needle down beside the bead hole. Pull the knot tight and remove the needle at the minute.

4. Continue adding beads one at a time, tying a new knot after each. Thread on the calotte and tie a loose overhand knot. Use the tapestry needle again to guide the knot inside the calotte. Trim the end and apply a little glue. Close the calotte with flat-nose pliers.

USING HALF-HITCH KNOTS

Bead stringing wire can't be knotted but if you like the way the beads hang you can still get the knotted look using this simple technique. The beads need a hole large enough to take both thread and wire.

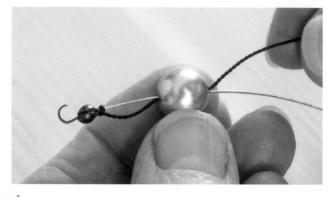

1. Secure beading thread and bead stringing wire into a calotte using a crimp (see the crimps technique) and thread the first bead on to the wire. Using a needle, pass the thread through this bead in the same direction.

2. Tie a half-hitch (see Tying Knots) using the beading thread over the bead stringing wire and pull up so that the knot is next to the bead. Repeat to the end then attach another calotte and fastening.

USING REEF (SQUARE) KNOTS

This technique is easier to work but the knots aren't quite as neat. It is ideal for necklaces and bracelets with chunkier beads.

1. Attach a calotte and fastening so that there is a double thread coming from the calotte and tie a reef knot (see Tying Knots). Pull the threads apart to tighten the knot close to the bead at each stage of tying.

2. Thread a needle on each end or work with a big-eye needle that is easy to thread after each knot. Pick up a bead by passing both threads through the hole in the same direction. Tie a reef knot again. Repeat to the end and add another calotte and fastening (see step 4 of Overhand Knots

SPACING WITH CRIMPS

Beads spaced on bead stringing wire have the appearance of floating because the beads are more prominent than the wire. A single strand is delicate but several strands give more impact. Secure a single wire using a crimp and loop and multiple strands in a calotte or tubular crimp fastening.

1. If you are starting with a bead near the fastening, begin by threading a crimp and fastening onto the bead stringing wire. Take the tail through the crimp and secure with crimp pliers. Add a bead over the tail and main wire, then a crimp. Hold it up slightly so that the bead and crimp are sitting side by side. Secure the crimp with flat-nose or crimp pliers.

2. Work out the spacing on the strand and mark the wire with a permanent marker where the beads will lie. Pick up another crimp and secure to one side so that the bead will cover the pen mark. Pick up a bead and another crimp. Secure as before.

3. Work down the strand, securing crimps either side of the bead each time. If you prefer not to mark the wire, you can fold a piece of paper over the wire then secure the next crimp butting up against the paper.

SPACING WITH GLUE

Illusion necklaces have beads strung on clear monofilament thread (Illusion cord). This is almost invisible and gives the appearance of beads floating in air. The beads can be spaced using crimps (see above) but are usually glued in position. Use a calotte or tubular crimp fastening to secure the strands of thread.

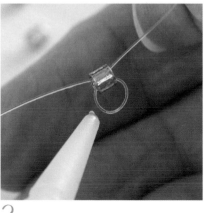

1. Pick up a seed bead and slide close to where you want it to be. Apply a drop of instant glue. Using a tapestry needle, slide the bead over the tiny drop of glue. Hold until the glue dries.

2. With larger seed beads, loop the thread through the bead again and slide along until the bead is in the correct position. Apply a drop of instant glue into the bead hole.

3. For heavy beads, pass the thread through the bead as before. Then take the tail through between the bead and the loop on the side and pull to form a half-hitch knot. Add a drop of instant glue and then tug the thread to hide the knot inside.

Thong, Cord and Rope

It can be challenging deciding how to finish jewellery made from thong, ribbons, cords and ropes. Basic findings can be utilitarian but new innovations like end caps in larger sizes are now easier to source.

USING SLIDING KNOTS

Ideal for casual jewellery or bracelets made from round thong or waxed cotton; allow an extra 20cm (8in) to accomodate the knots and simple slide fastening. You can use this technique to make bracelets and necklaces adjustable.

1. Arrange the cords so they are parallel and the tails point in opposite directions. Pass one end under the other cord and then work an overhand knot (see Tying Knots).

2. Repeat with the other end, tying the knot so the tail is facing in the opposite direction to the first knot. Pull the knots apart to shorten and away from each other to lengthen.

ADDING FASTENINGS

Most findings for bead stringing are too small for cords and thong as the bulky material is difficult to knot neatly. Choose one of these findings so that you can attach a fastening.

1. SPRING COIL ENDS
For rattail, ribbon, thick round thong and multiple thinner cords. Feed the cord right through the spiral and trim the end; move the spiral slightly to hide the raw edge and squeeze the bottom ring only with snipe-nosed pliers.

2. CORD END
For waxed cotton and round leather thong. Apply a little jewellery glue to the end of the cord; insert the cord and wipe away any excess glue. Leave to dry.

3. THONG (FOLD OVER) ENDS
For faux suede, flat leather thong and thicker cords. Slot the faux suede between the lugs on the finding; flatten one side down and then the other with snipe- or flat-nose pliers.

4. CRIMP END
For waxed cotton and round leather thong. Insert the end of the cord or waxed cotton into the finding and squeeze the last few millimetres with flat-nose pliers to flatten and secure.

5. RIBBON CLAMP
For ribbon and wider macramé bands. Use a clamp that is slightly wider than the ribbon or fold in the ribbon ends slightly. Apply a little glue to the inside, position the ribbon and then squeeze flat with snipe-nose pliers.

End caps are larger and ideal for ropes and thick cord.

Stringing is usually thought of as strands of beads hanging down around the neck, but you can string beads through other materials to create more impact. The necklace shape is created first by plaiting and knotting chain and leather thong together. Then the beads are strung onto bead stringing wire as it is woven through to embellish and support the base necklace. See the Projects chapter for step-by-step instructions for making the **Briar and Bramble Necklace**.

MAKING ROPES

There are lots of cords and ropes available to buy but it can be difficult to find the right colour and thickness for a particular piece of jewellery. Yarn and embroidery cotton are suitable for making thinner ropes but if you want a substantial, attractive rope try satin cord (mouse or rattail). You can twist the cord using a cord maker or twist shorter lengths by hand.

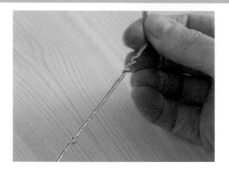

1. Cut a length of satin cord more than twice the length you require – 1m (1yd) will make, approximately, a 45cm (16in) rope. Hold shorter lengths stretched out between your hands. Twist one end in the same direction as the light twist on the rattail. Keep twisting until the rope begins to twist back against itself.

2. Fold the cord in half letting the rope twist up randomly. Hold the two ends together firmly and run the rope between your finger and thumb to smooth out any kinks. Wrap fine wire around the cut ends to secure.

3. For longer, thicker ropes you can use a cord maker or hand drill. Secure the ends in a clamp or tie to a heavy object. Loop the doubled cord over the cup hook and turn the handle until the rope begins to turn back on itself. Fold over and run between finger and thumb to smooth out the kinks.

USING A KUMIHIMO TOOL

Japanese braiding makes very attractive rope for jewellery; the ends can be finished easily by glueing into an end cap. You can make a four, eight or 12 strands. There are many different patterns but this simple pattern for eight strands will get you started. Cut four lengths of cord twice the length you require, say 80cm (31½in) for a 19cm (7¼in) bracelet.

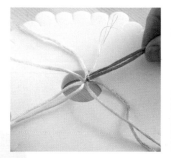

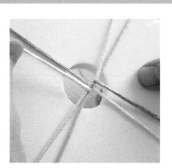

1. Tie the cords together in the middle with a piece of wire or thread. Position the tie in the middle of the disc. Spread the cords out in a cross. Tuck one cord either side of these four corners.

2. Bring the top right cord down to bottom right and tuck in the new slot. Take the bottom left cord up to top left and tuck in the new slot.

3. Rotate the disc a quarter turn anti-clockwise and begin the process again. Repeat from step 2 until the rope is the length you require.

4. If you want, you can add a weight to the end of the rope to keep it in place and help make even braiding.

TYING KNOTS

There are several simple knots that are used in jewellery making that will ensure your pieces remain intact and fastenings firmly attached. For extra security, add a drop of jewellery glue on the knots and leave to dry before trimming the tails.

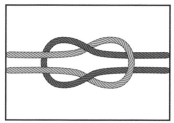

REEF (SQUARE) KNOT

A basic knot for two threads of equal thickness. It is fairly secure but can be loosened by tugging on one end. To tie, pass the left thread over the right and tuck under. Then pass the right thread over the left and tuck under the left thread and through the gap in the middle of the knot.

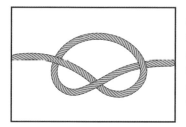

OVERHAND KNOT

Use to tie a bundle of threads together or to tie a knot in a small calotte (see Adding Fastenings). To tie, simply cross the tail over the main thread to make a small loop, then pass the tail under the thread and back through the loop. You can manoeuvre the knot into position with a tapestry needle.

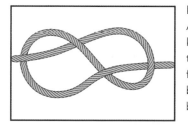

FIGURE OF EIGHT KNOT

An alternative to an overhand knot for calottes, this makes a larger knot that is less likely to pull through the hole in the hinge or side. To tie, cross the tail in front of the main thread and hold between your finger and thumb so that the loop is facing towards you. Take the tail behind the main thread and pass through the loop from the front. Pull both ends to tighten.

LARK'S HEAD KNOT

Use to attach cords and thongs to rings and pendant beads. To tie, fold the cord in half and take the loop you have made through the ring from the reverse side. Pass the tails through the loop and pull up to tighten. To make a reverse lark's head knot, pass the loop through the ring from the front to back and complete the knot by passing the tails through the loop again.

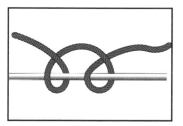

HALF-HITCH KNOT

Generally used to secure threads in bead stitching or when stringing beads with thread. To tie, take the needle behind a thread between beads and pull through leaving a loop. Pass the needle back through the loop and pull up to make the half-hitch. Work a second half-hitch a few beads along for extra security, applying a drop of jewellery glue before trimming the tail.

Wire

Wire-based jewellery is one of the most satisfying crafts to learn as the techniques are easy but you can produce stunning results in a minimal amount of time. This chapter covers all the basic techniques, explains how to use wire products and looks at more advanced wirework using precious metal wire.

Basic Techniques

You will need a basic set of jewellery tools to begin. The four essential pliers – round-nose, flat-nose, snipe-nose and wire cutters – can be used to make most wire work and jewellery items.

STRAIGHTENING WIRE

Wire is generally sold in coils and reels and as a result is curved when unwound. This curve can be useful when making coils but often it is better to begin with straight wire.

1. To take a gentle curve out of craft wire, fold a piece of tissue and pull the wire through between your finger and thumb and exert pressure to straighten out the curve. You can also run the wire through nylon jaw pliers.

2. To straighten wire with lots of kinks along the length, either secure one end in a vice or use two pairs of flat-nose pliers and pull the wire as hard as you can in opposite directions.

CUTTING WIRE

You can use strong craft scissors to cut very fine wires (0.2–0.3mm) but it is better to invest in a pair of good quality wire cutters. Side cutters have a flat and an angled side but more expensive flush cutters cut both ends of the wire straight.

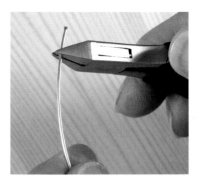

1. Cut with the flat side of the wire cutters towards the work to get a straight cut on the end of the wire. Make sure the flat side of the pliers is perpendicular to the wire so that the cut is straight and not angled.

2. When cutting a wire that crosses over another wire, use the very tips of the blades to get as close as possible to the crossover point. Hold the flat side of the wire cutters next to the work.

BENDING WIRE

You need to be quite firm to get wire to bend where you want. Choose flat- or snipe-nose pliers to bend wire at an angle. Avoid pliers with a serrated surface that will damage the wire.

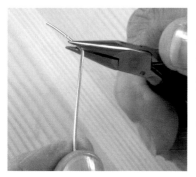

1. Hold the wire firmly with the flat-nose pliers so that the edge of the jaw is exactly where you want the wire to bend. Rotate the pliers to create a particular angle.

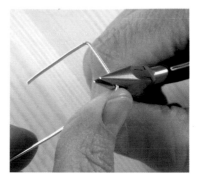

2. To create a right-angle, hold the tail of the wire and push up against the jaws of the pliers with your thumb.

TWISTING WIRE

Twist wire to create texture and add body to the wire so that it supports the weight of a bead or holds its shape better. A twisted wire looks more delicate than thicker craft wire and so is popular for tiaras.

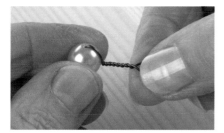

1. Use a bead to give you leverage for twisting the wire. Hold the bead between your finger and thumb and roll it round and round until the wire is evenly twisted along its length.

2. Rather than making a single twist, create short branches by only twisting for a short length and then adding a bead to one tail and twisting to make the branch. Add other branches as required.

3. If you are using thicker wire and find it easier to twist the wire rather than the bead, splay the wires out at right-angles so that you can exert a more even pressure to make a neater twist.

MAKING TWISTED WIRE

Lengths of twisted wire can be used to give a textured appearance to jewellery and wirework or to make decorative jump rings.

1. A cord maker or hand drill is ideal for twisting lengths of wire. Loop the wire over the hook, secure the ends in a vice and turn the handle until it is twisted evenly along the length.

2. Take care when releasing the wire as it can spring. You can use an electric drill if it has a slow speed setting. Simply fit a cup hook in the chubb instead of a drill bit.

Coiling

Coils of wire add a decorative touch to jewellery making. Use round-nose pliers to begin and flat-nose pliers with smooth jaws to bend the wire in a loose or tight coil.

LOOSE COIL

1. To begin, make a small loop at the end of the wire using round-nose pliers. Then hold the wire at the very end of the pliers and bend the wire round until it touches the tail again.

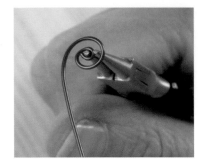

2. To make the coil, hold the wire a few centimetres (1¼in) from the pliers and bend the wire gently round, moving the pliers in the loop until it is the size you require.

TIGHT COIL

1. Using round-nose pliers make a small 'U' shape on the end of the wire rather than a loop.

2. Hold the 'U' sideways in flat-nose pliers and bend the straight wire round. Move the tiny coil around a few millimetres (⅛in). Bend the wire round against the loop. Keep rotating the coil and bending the wire around until it is the size required.

CAGED BEAD

Wrapping wire around beads is an elegant way to assimilate the beads into wirework jewellery.

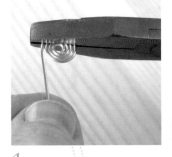

1. Cut a 20cm (8in) length of 1mm (19swg) wire. Make a small 'U' shape on one end with round-nose pliers and begin to make a tight coil.

2. Coil the other end of the wire and wind both coils into the centre so that they are the same size and form an 'S' shape.

3. Push the centre of each coil with round-nose pliers to form two domes. Bend the domes towards each other to form an oval cage.

4. Use pliers to open the cage slightly and slide a bead inside. Adjust the coils with pliers. You can bend the wire with pliers to tighten the cage against the bead.

SPIRAL BEADS

Use this spring technique to make delightful wire beads. You can make short or long beads depending on the length of the spring. Try different thicknesses and colours of wire to make delicate or chunky beads.

 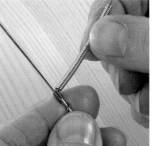 

1. Wrap 0.6mm (24 swg) wire around a thin knitting needle (size 0000) or 1.2mm (18swg) wire to make a 4–5cm (1½-2in) spring. Remove the spring and trim the ends.

2. Leaving a short tail for leverage, wrap 0.7mm (22swg) wire around the knitting needle four or five times. Trim the long tail to about 20cm (8in) and slide the long spring down to the knitting needle.

3. Holding the short tail for leverage, begin to wrap the spring around the knitting needle. You will need to push the spring down as you wrap, catching the last coil with your nail to stop it sliding up the wire.

4. Once the spring is wrapped around the knitting needle, wrap the core wire around four or five times and then slide the spiral bead off. Trim the ends of wire neatly.

Spiral beads can be used with other beads to make different pieces of jewellery. Try making beads to fit inside large, square donut beads, like in this pretty bag charm.

WRAPPED BEADS

Open out a spiral bead and position it around a large bead to make an attractive wrapped bead.

1. Make a spiral bead as above. Loosen the spiral by holding each end and turning the ends in opposite directions.

2. Slip a suitable bead into the loose coil and adjust to fit. Feed an eyepin through the holes in the spiral and bead. Trim the end to 7mm (⅛in) and make a loop with round nose pliers (see the Plain Loop technique).

PLAIN LOOP

Make a plain loop on a headpin to create a bead dangle. Headpins are available in several lengths; choose a length to suit the size of beads. You will need 0.5 or 0.6mm (24–25swg) thickness headpins to make a secure plain loop that doesn't pull apart.

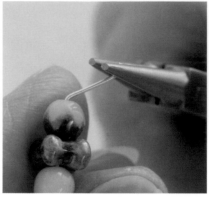

1. Pick up the beads required on the headpin. Trim the headpin to 7–10mm (⅜–½in) and bend over at a right-angle using snipe-nose pliers. The length you cut from the top bead will depend on the thickness of the wire and the size of the loop required.

2. Hold the tip of the wire with round-nose pliers and rotate the pliers to bend the wire part-way around the tip. The distance you hold the wire down from the top of the pliers will determine the size of the loop.

3. Reposition the pliers by flipping your wrist, then continue to rotate the wire around until the tip touches the wire again and the loop is in the middle.

BEAD LINK

Bead links have a loop at each end with one or more beads in the middle. They can be joined together to make earrings, bracelets or necklaces, used to join lengths of chain, or added to a bead dangle to make a beaded pendant.

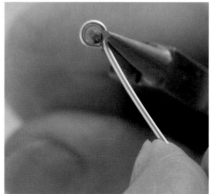

1. To make the first loop, hold the wire or a trimmed headpin about 6mm (¼in) from the top of round-nose pliers. Make sure the tip of the wire is level with the jaws and not jutting out.

2. Bend the wire around the jaws by rotating the pliers until the tip touches the wire again. Change the position of the pliers and bend the wire back slightly to straighten the loop. This is known as 'breaking the neck'.

3. Feed the beads you require onto the end of the wire. Trim the wire to 7mm and then follow Plain Loop, steps 2 and 3 to create a loop on the other end of the bead link. Hold one loop and use snipe-nose pliers to rotate until both face in the same direction.

Bead dangles, made from headpins, are a great way to add interest to a plain string of beads. Add a bead link and a longer bead dangle to the middle of the string and you will create a completely different style of necklace. The Y-shape necklace is one of the most flattering styles as it enhances your décolletage. See the Projects chapter for step-by-step instructions for making the **Ice-cream Sundae Necklace**.

WRAPPED LOOP DANGLE

Wrapping creates a stronger and more secure connection than a plain loop. It is ideal for finer wires, or for more precious beads or charms that you don't want to lose. Wrapped loops are also useful for beads with slightly larger holes.

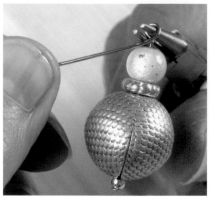

1. Use longer headpins to allow for the wrapping – you will need at least 3cm (1¼in) of wire above the last bead. Pick up the beads required and, using snipe-nose pliers, hold the wire above the bead, leaving a small gap, and bend at a right-angle.

2. Hold the wire close to the bend with round-nose pliers and wrap the tail all the way round to form a loop. Bring the wire right round so that it is at right-angles to the wire inside the beads.

3. Hold the loop flat in snipe-nose pliers and wind the wire tail around the stem covering the gap between the loop and the bead. If you find it difficult to wrap the wire by hand, use flat-nose pliers for more purchase. Trim the tail.

WRAPPED LOOP CHAIN

You can make a longer wire wrap section to make a decorative chain (five or six coils is the maximum), or even wrap the end of the headpin around the bead to make a more decorative dangle.

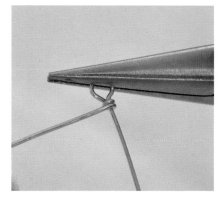

1. To make the first wrapped loop, use round-nose pliers to create a loop at least 3cm (1¼in) from the end of the wire. Hold the loop in snipe-nose pliers and 'break the neck'. With the tail wire horizontal, wind it 2–3 times around the main wire. Trim the tail and tuck the end of the wire in with snipe-nose pliers.

2. Add the beads and make a wrapped loop after the beads as described in the wrapped loop dangle above. Begin the next wrapped loop link but only pre-form the second loop. Insert the previous bead link into the loop.

3. Hold the loop you are making in snipe-nose pliers and then wind the tail around the main wire to complete the wrapping. Trim the tail as before. Repeat all steps to make a chain.

WRAPPING A DROP BEAD

Briolettes and other pendant or drop beads with a top horizontal hole use a different wrapping technique. Use 0.6mm (24 swg) wire or a harder, thinner wire such as 0.4mm (27swg) if the hole in the briolette is too small.

1. Thread the tail of the wire through the hole in the briolette leaving about 12mm (½in) sticking out the other side. Bend both the tail and the main wire up towards the top of the briolette.

2. Using snipe-nose pliers, bend the short tail back just above the top of the bead. Repeat with the main wire. Using wire cutters, trim the wire tail about 3mm (⅛in) about the bend.

3. Grasp both the tail and main wire with snipe-nose pliers and bend the main wire back to create the section for wrapping. Trim the tail to ⅛in (3mm). As with the wrapped loop dangle (see above) wrap the wire around round-nose pliers to make a loop.

4. Hold the loop firmly with snipe-nose pliers and wrap the wire around the neck two or three times until you reach the bend in the wires. Trim neatly with side cutters, using snipe-nose pliers to push in the end if required.

Wrapped loop links are needed to create the links in this necklace as the brass wire is too soft to hold its shape for a plain loop.

Jump Rings

Jump rings are round- or oval-shaped pieces of wire with a gap for opening or closing. They are generally used to attach findings or join elements together but can be used in their own right to make stunning chain maille jewellery. Ideally work with two flat-nose or snipe-nose pliers but you can use round-nose with a pair of flat-nose pliers.

OPENING AND CLOSING

1. Hold the jump ring with two pairs of flat-nose pliers; to open the ring, bring one pair of pliers towards you. Reverse the action to close.

2. You can temper (harden) the jump ring by opening and closing the ring a couple of times. Alternatively, when using silver wire, tap the jump rings lightly a few times to harden using a rubber hammer and block (see Hammering Wire).

3. To tension the jump rings so the ends butt together, use pliers to push the ends slightly so that they overlap on one side and then the other. Pull back and the ends will spring together.

TWO IN TWO CHAIN

Linking jump rings together to make chain or jewellery is known as chain maille. Have a supply of open and closed rings ready to make this chain; link together in pairs or even threes to make a more ornate chain.

1. Open two jump rings and loop one through four jump rings. Close the ring with two pairs of pliers. Attach a second jump ring through the four jump rings in the same way.

2. Hold so that you have a chain of pairs of jump rings (three to start). Pick up two closed rings on an open ring and loop through the top pair on the chain. Close this ring and add another through the same four rings. Repeat until the chain is the length you require.

FLOWER CHAIN

Interlink three jump rings together to make little flower shapes and then join all the flowers together to make a pretty chain with jump rings.

1. Join two rings together. Open a third ring and loop it through where the first two overlap. Close the ring.

2. Group the rings into a flower shape. If the flower shape isn't compact, like the sample on the right, you need to flop the loose ring so that they all nestle close together, like the sample on the left.

3. Make several flowers. Loop an open jump ring through two flower shapes and close. Pick up further flowers one at a time with a jump ring, loop through the end flower in the chain and close.

MAKING JUMP RINGS

If you need a particular thickness of wire and size of ring for a chain maille project, it is easy to make your own jump rings. For large quantities, you can invest in a jump ring maker.

1. Choose a mandrel or rod of the required diameter (see Other Equipment). Hold the end of the wire at one end and wrap tightly around the rod.

2. Slide the wound spring off the rod. Pull the spring open slightly by hand or with two pairs of pliers. Use wire cutters to trim one end of the wire straight.

3. Line up the pliers with the first cut so that the cut end is inside the hollow side of the pliers and snip to make the jump ring. Turn the pliers round and trim the new end each time with the flat edge of the wire cutters before cutting the next jump ring.

BYZANTINE CHAIN

This chain, also known as King's Braid and Idiot's Delight, requires you use an appropriate wire gauge and jump ring size combination. If the gauge is too small the chain will be loose; too large and it will be difficult to insert the required number of rings. Suggested combinations are: 1.2mm (18 swg) 4.8mm inner diameter; 1mm (19swg) 4mm ID; 0.8mm (21swg) 3.2mm ID and 0.6mm (24swg) 2.5mm ID. For 1mm wire you will need roughly 20–24 rings per 2.5cm (1in).

1. Begin with three pairs of jump rings (purple, fuchsia and pink) made into the two in two chain (step 1) and put a twist tie from an 8cm (3in) length of wire through two end rings (purple) in the chain. Be sure to close each ring flush before continuing.

2. Hold the twist tie between finger and thumb and let the top two pink rings (5 and 6) fall down, one on either side, against the purple rings (1 and 2). Hold the pink rings against the side of the chain and the middle pair of fuchsia rings (3 and 4) will be angled open into a knot formation.

3. Add two more purple rings (7 and 8) through the top end of the pink rings (5 and 6) to secure the knot formation of the chain.

4. Add two more pairs of rings, fuchsia and then pink (9 and 10 plus 11 and 12) to make the 2+2+2 sequence in step 1.

5. Fold back the last pair of pink rings (11 and 12) and hold them between finger and thumb as in step 2. Hold these rings flat and the middle pair of fuchsia rings (9 and 10) in the sequence will be angled open again in a knot formation.

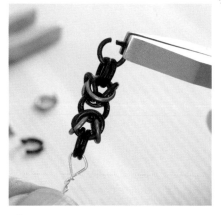

6. Alternate Byzantine chain formations are a mirror image of the first sequence so you need to rotate the chain 90 degrees to see the knot formation. Add two more purple rings (13 and 14) through the top end of the pink rings (11 and 12); use as a 'bead' to make the necklace opposite or repeat from step 4 until the chain is the length you require.

Byzantine chain maille is one of the most attractive weaves for jewellery. It looks intricate but is actually an easy pattern to learn. It can be worked as a solid rope but the individual units work well when separated with beads too. This design, which could be worked as a bracelet instead, has jet black magatamas added on jump rings between the individual units. For a finishing touch, string one or two Cosmic rings. See the Projects chapter for step-by-step instructions for making the **Cosmic Links** necklace.

Making Findings

Using basic wire working techniques, it is easy to make different findings from simple jump rings to more advanced fastenings for your jewellery. You can use plated or enamelled jewellery wires to begin with, then make your own precious metal findings.

JEWELLERY FASTENINGS

Use round- and flat-nose pliers to make a simple hook-and-eye fastening for necklaces and bracelets.

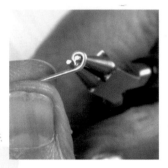

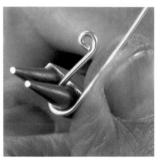

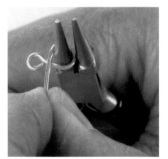

1. Form a tiny loop at the end of a 5cm (2in) piece of 1.2mm (18 swg) wire using the very tip of round-nose pliers.

2. Hold the wire at the base of the plier's jaws about 12mm (½in) away from the loop and wrap the wire around the jaws until the loop touches the wire once more.

3. Grasp the wire near the base of the pliers. Bend the wire round to make a loop at right-angles to the hook. Reposition the pliers and bend the loop back to straighten (break the neck).

4. To make the other part of the fastening, make an eyepin with a 4cm (1½in) length of 1.2mm (18 swg) wire. Make a larger loop with the other tail of the eyepin and straighten to make a figure of eight.

EARRING WIRES

Make a pair of contemporary earring wires then learn how to use hammers to shape and harden the metal.

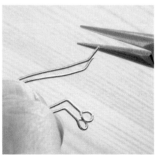

1. Cut two 6.5cm (2½in) pieces of 0.8mm (21swg) of half-hard silver wire. Make a small plain loop on the end of each wire using round-nose pliers then 'break the neck' to make an eyepin loop.

2. Hold the wires and loops together. Bend with flat nose pliers 5mm (¼in) from the loops. Wrap around a mandrel or round-nose pliers to make the curved shape of the earring wires.

3. Reposition and bend again around the mandrel to create the bottom curve. Hold the wires together and trim the ends about 4mm (⅛in) from the bend.

4. Smooth any jagged edges on the ends of the wire using a file then round off using a cup bur (see Other Equipment). The earring wires can be hammered for a professional finish (see below).

HAMMERING WIRE

Wire is hammered to flatten, create texture, straighten or harden (temper) it. It is easier to create loops with a soft wire and then harden them with a hard plastic mallet, which, unlike a metal hammer, will not make the wire brittle. A chasing hammer has a smooth, domed head that makes it easier to taper wire by hammering at a slight angle. It is used to flatten wire ends and parts of findings for a more professional finish.

• Use a hard rubber hammer to straighten kinks in wire before beginning, or neaten shaped wire as you make findings. Hammer on a rubber block.

• Gently tapping jump rings and other looped findings a few times causes a physical reaction in the wire that hardens it.

• Place one end of the wire on a steel block and tap several times with a chasing hammer until flat. Use the flattened wire as a headpin, to begin coiling or to make a small loop on the end of wire.

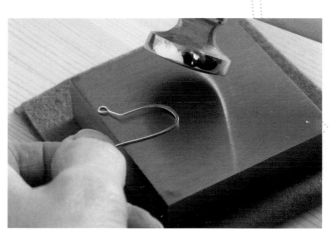

• Flatten the rounded part of earring wires with a chasing hammer to create a decorative finish. You may need to reshape with flat-nose pliers.

• Use the ball pen end of the chasing hammer to create tiny dents on wire to make an interesting texture.

Making Rings

Rings can be made in a range of styles by wrapping wire around a mandrel. You can use a shaped ring mandrel to get the size right but you may find it easier and more accurate to wrap wire around a straight sided rod or tube of the right diameter. Use a soft wire to wrap the rings; harder wires will be very difficult to wrap neatly.

BASIC WIRE RING

This style of ring has the wire running through the bead horizontally and is suitable for flatter beads, either rectangular, oval or round.

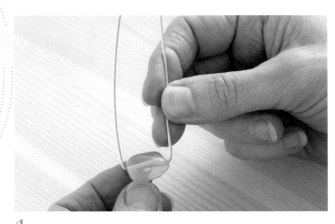

1. Cut a 40cm (15in) length of 1mm (19swg) wire and pick up a flattish, large bead that fits across the width of your finger. Bend both ends up so that the bead is in the middle of the wire.

2. Hold the bead against a ring mandrel at the mark for your size of ring and wrap the wire around and back across the front of the mandrel.

3. Wrap the bottom wire around the bead until it is back where you started. Repeat with the wire at the other side so that the wires end up pointing in opposite directions.

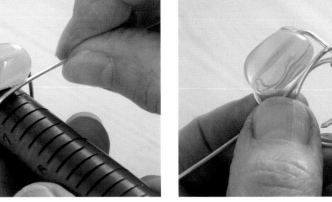

4. Take the ring off the mandrel. Wrap the wires at each side around the band two or three times. Repeat at the other side and trim the tail neatly.

WIRE WRAPPED RING

The wire holding the bead goes vertically through the bead. Briolette beads make a ring that sits fairly low on your hand or you can use a square or round bead to make a statement ring.

1. Cut a 40cm (15in) length of 1mm (19swg) wire and wrap the wire twice around the mandrel at the right mark for your ring size so that one wire tail is longer than the other. Bend the longer wire around the other.

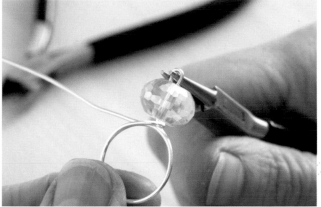

2. Slide the bead down the upright wire. Trim 7mm (⅜in) from the bead. Use round-nose pliers to create a small loop.

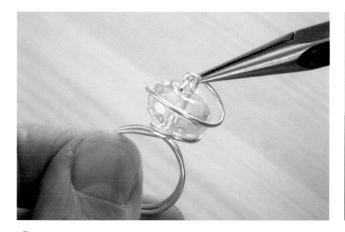

3. Wrap the other wire around the bead in a gentle spiral. Feed the end through the loop at the top of the bead. Trim if necessary and coil the end attractively.

4. Cut a length of 0.4mm (27swg) silver wire. Hold the centre behind the ring. Wrap the finer wire around the ring back. Tuck the tail through the last few coils on the inside and then pull taut. Trim neatly.

Working With Chain

Chain is available in a variety of sizes and materials. More expensive chain has soldered links but the majority of jewellery chain has open links. To cut chain, measure the length required, then cut through the next link on one side. If it is thick or made from hard wire, cut through both sides so that the link falls away.

JOINING CHAIN TO FASTENINGS

Attach fastenings or other jewellery findings using small jump rings.

1. Open the jump ring with two pairs of pliers, loop through the last link of the chain and the fastening, then close the jump ring.

2. Bead links and dangles hang better on a charm bracelet if they are attached to one side of the chain. Lay the chain down on the work surface or a beading mat so that it is flat and untwisted. Attach jump rings or charms to one side on alternate links.

THREADING WITH RIBBON

A wide, sheer ribbon will bunch out through the links giving a very soft appearance. Depending on the style of chain you can miss links or weave through every one.

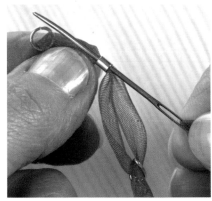

1. Loop the ribbon through a large eye needle and weave it back and forwards through the links. Pull the ribbon through the links leaving a long tail at each end.

2. Thread the ribbon tail through a large tube crimp, then a jump ring and back through the crimp. Thread it through the last link in the chain and back through the crimp again.

3. Pull the ribbon with both ends until you manoeuvre the chain, crimp and jump rings close together. Repeat at both ends of the chain, squeeze the crimp to flatten and then trim the ribbon tails.

THREADING WITH ELASTIC

If you thread elastic through the links of chain it will scrunch up to create a very textured effect. The links can be embellished in the same way as a charm bracelet.

1. Loop a double length of elastic thread through a large eye needle and weave it back and forwards through the links.

2. Decide on the size of the bracelet. Tie the threads together with a couple of reef knots (see Tying Knots) or secure the ends by passing both ends through two crimps from opposite ends and flatten with pliers.

Short lengths of chain threaded onto the bead stringing wire scrunch up to create texture in this seahorse charm.

ANTIQUING WIREWORK

Jewellery and wirework components can be artificially aged to give it an antique look in minutes. The technique works on silver, copper or brass wire. You can antique jewellery with most beads attached although bone, ivory and polymer clay are not suitable.

1. Working in a well-ventilated area, drop a chunk or few drops of liver of sulphur into a small bowl of hot (not boiling) water and stir until completely dissolved. Use pliers to lower the jewellery into the solution until it is submerged. Leave for a few minutes and then lift out. Rinse the jewellery out in a bowl of luke warm water. Pat dry with kitchen towel and leave for several hours or overnight to dry completely.

2. Protect the work surface with kitchen towel. Polish the jewellery with 0000 steel wool, polishing in one direction only for best results. Use a stiff wire brush to clean out bits of steel wool trapped in any crevices. Polish the jewellery with a soft cloth, or you can use a chemically treated cloth like a Sunshine Cloth™ to speed up the process.

Bead Stitches

Often called needle weaving, bead stitching is used to make pieces of beaded fabric, which can be incorporated into many styles of jewellery. Flat bands make pretty bracelets, circular forms can make attractive medallions for brooches or bib-style necklaces and tubular versions make fabulous ropes and cords.

Getting Started

Beading needles and some sewing needles like sharps, which have a small eye, are suitable for bead stitching. Choose a size 10 or even a size 13 if the needle has to pass through the beads several times. As a guide, thread size 11 beads with a size 10 needle and size 15 beads with the size 13 needle. There are lots of different threads suitable for bead stitching (see Choosing Threads) and, to some extent, the choice is personal.

*Nymo was the original **multifilament beading thread** but new types such as KO and S-lon are popular too. These threads are available in a range of colours and useful for techniques where the thread is likely to show.*

Threads can be ready-waxed or conditioned or you can add the conditioner yourself. This helps to prevent the thread tangling and can also keep stitching tight.

***Fine braided threads** such as Dandyline and Fireline are less likely to stretch and so are really good for firm techniques like bezels where you want the beads to create a structure.*

JOINING ON ANOTHER THREAD

This technique is suitable for all bead stitching. Work with as long a thread as possible to minimize the number of joins. It is possible to join a thread by weaving back and forwards through the beads but much more secure to work a half-hitch knot or two as you go (see Tying Knots).

1. When joining a new thread, select a column of beads directly below where the old thread emerges. Take the needle with the new thread in between two beads about eight or nine beads from where the old thread ends and out about four beads further up.

2. Pass the needle under threads between two beads and pull it out through the loop of thread to work a half-hitch. Go up through the next few beads to bring the needle out the same bead where the old thread emerges.

3. To sew in the old thread, take the needle and thread back down through several beads. Pass the needle under threads between two beads and pull it out through the loop of thread to work a half-hitch. Take the needle through another few beads and either trim the tail or work a second half-hitch for extra security.

*Uses a **thread zapper** (see Equipment) to sear tiny ends for a better finish.*

Beaded Ropes

Beaded ropes and cords are a versatile way to work with bead stitching to make jewellery. Although often associated with bracelets, you can use long ropes to make necklaces and lariats, short lengths for earrings or even stitch lengths into hoops to make a chain link.

SPIRAL TWIST

Spiral twist is the basic rope and a perennial favourite. It is one of the strongest spiral techniques because the thread goes through the core beads several times as you work the beading. Use a contrast colour, either lighter or darker, for the core beads to create the most attractive effect.

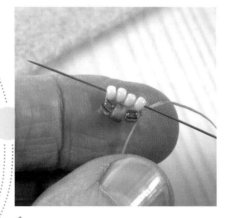  

1. Pick up four size 11 opaque seed beads, then a sequence of a size 11 transparent seed bead, a size 8 bead and a size 11 transparent seed bead and tie into a circle. Pass the needle through the four opaque seed beads again.

2. Pick up one opaque and the three seed beads sequence. Take the needle through the last opaque seed beads on the spiral. Pull the thread up and then take the needle through the last opaque seed bead added.

3. Repeat step 2 to add a second loop of beads. Continue repeating step 2, making sure that the loops lie right next to each other. After four or five repeats the spiral effect will be quite obvious. Join new threads as required and secure the ends as shown in the Joining on Another Thread technique.

Vary the technique by altering the style and number of beads that step up around the core. Using larger beads for the core creates a completely different effect.

*This style of **spiral twist** requires no additional finishing. There is a single thread at each end, which can be used to sew a fastening or add a bead loop to one end and a bead or beaded toggle at the other end.*

DOUBLE CORE SPIRAL

This variation of the basic spiral technique uses large beads for the core, which remains on the outside with bugles and loops of seed beads on the outside, making a delightful textured and supple rope. This example uses double Delicas, which are large size 8 beads.

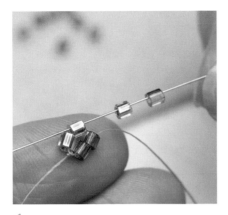

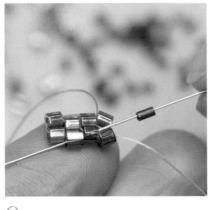

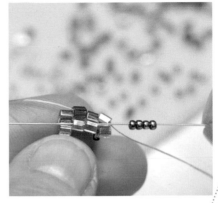

1. Using a 2m (2yd) length of thread with the beading needle, pick up two cinnamon double Delicas and two blue double Delicas, drop down to 50cm (18in) from the end and tie in a circle. Take the needle through the two cinnamon beads again and add another cinnamon and blue bead. Take the needle through the blue then the cinnamon beads again ready to add another pair of beads.

2. Pick up a cinnamon and blue double Delica and pass the needle down through two of the blue beads already added. Pick up a 3mm bugle and take the needle across and up through two cinnamon beads. Turn the beading over to the other side.

3. Pick up four size 11 steel blue seed beads. These will sit diagonally across the block of four Delicas below where the thread is emerging, so count down two blue Delicas and take the needle back up only through these two beads, coming out between the top two blue Delicas.

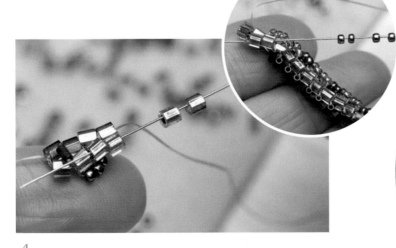

4. Turn the beading over and take the needle across and back through the top cinnamon Delica ready to begin the sequence again. Repeat from step 2 using size 11 light sapphire seed beads on the next repeat instead of steel blue and aqua beads on the one after. Repeat the sequence, using the three different colours of seed beads in rotation. Continue working the bead rope until it is the length required.

Bead ropes can be made into small circles or loops and joined to create a chain. Whichever technique you use, sew the ends together and fill in with beads to create a seamless join.

TUBULAR HERRINGBONE STITCH

In herringbone stitch, the beads are added two at a time forming the distinctive 'stacks' that are much more obvious, and the stitch easier to learn, if you work with different colours of beads in adjacent pairs. Use only four, six or eight beads to create a rope and 12 or more to create a tube. Begin with a double row of ladder stitch, shown here.

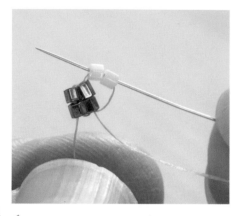

1. Pick up four dark beads and go back through all the beads and pull up. Pick up two light beads and take the needle through the last two dark beads and then the light beads again.

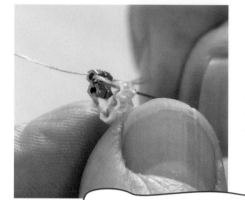

2. Continue adding two beads at a time, changing the colours every four beads to make a six-bead wide, two-bead high strip. Join the two ends together by taking the needle back through the first two beads and the last two beads to emerge at the opposite side to the tail thread.

The bead colour order depends on which way you turn the ladder stitch before sewing the ends together.

STRAIGHT HERRINGBONE STITCH

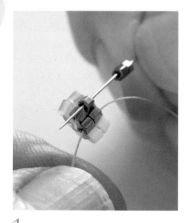

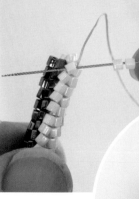

1. Make a ladder stitch base (see above) then begin the herringbone stitch. The thread should be coming out of the top of the band. *Pick up two beads the same colour as the bead where the thread is emerging and take the needle back down through the next bead along.

2. Pull the thread up so that the two beads sit side by side on top of the stack. Bring the needle up through the first bead in the next stack. Repeat from* until you reach the first stack again. The beads will all be the same level and so you need to 'step up' through two beads rather than just one so that the thread is emerging from the next stack along ready for the next round.

3. Finish the round and step up again. Repeat from * until the rope or tube is the length required. After a few more rounds you will begin to see the distinctive 'v' shape of herringbone stitch.

*Create an attractively textured rope with **bugles** and **cylinder beads** to make a pair of earrings.*

TWISTED HERRINGBONE STITCH

This variation of tubular herringbone is created by a simple alteration in the way the thread is routed through the beads, which causes the bead stack to tilt to one side and then spiral round as you add further rows.

Triangle beads work well with herringbone stitch and the twisted version is no exception. Each bead sits with a slightly different surface facing forward to create an interesting texture and the petrol finish introduces a variety of colours.

1. Begin with a ladder stitch base (see tubular herringbone stitch) and join the ends together by going through the end pairs of beads twice. Work two rounds of straight tubular herringbone stitch (see above) keeping the colour sequence the same as the ladder stitch base.

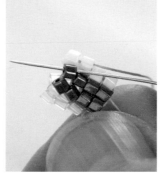

2. To begin the next round and create the twist, rather than stepping up through two beads, take the needle through the top bead only on the next stack.

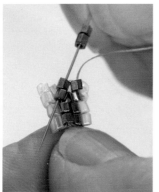

3. Pick up two beads to match the stack and take the needle back down through the next two beads. Pull the thread taut and you will see the beads beginning to tilt to one side.

4. Take the needle through the top bead on the next stack and pick up two beads, then take the needle back down through the next two beads. Repeat. As you are spiralling, there is no step up – simply keep repeating the 'two down, one up' until the rope is the length required.

EMBELLISHING HERRINGBONE

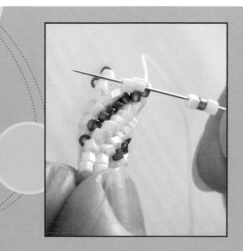

- It is easy to embellish either version of herringbone stitch further by adding another bead on each stitch. Simply pick up a small seed bead between the usual two beads on each stack and complete the stitch in the usual way.

- Herringbone stitch works well with beads of different sizes in each stack. A particularly attractive twisted rope can be made using alternate magatamas and seed beads.

Tubular Netting

Netting worked as a tube makes an attractive tyre-like rope. All netting bead stitches are worked with a combination of 'shared' and 'bridge' beads. The shared beads link adjacent rounds of beads; the bridge beads are strung between the shared beads. The thread passes through every second shared bead in each round to create the open netting effect.

NETTING ROPE

In this example you add five beads at a time (four bridge and one shared bead). You can vary the diameter of the tube so long as there is an odd number of three or more shared beads in the base circle.

 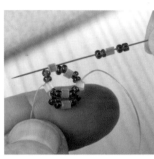  

1. Pick up one shared (pink satin) bead and two bridge (plum seed) beads. Repeat until there are 15 beads on the thread. Tie the thread in a circle, leaving a long tail and pass the needle through the first (pink satin) bead again.

2. *Pick up two bridge beads, a shared bead and two bridge beads. Miss the next shared bead and pass the needle through the next one in the circle. Repeat from * once more so that there are two netting loops coming off the circle.

3. For the third loop, pick up two bridge beads, a shared bead and two bridge beads. Pass the needle through the shared bead on the next loop. Repeat this step to add another two or three loops.

4. Choose a mandrel (see the Equipment section) that fits snugly through the initial loop and insert through the tubular netting. Pull the thread up until the beads are taut and then continue adding loops as before until the rope is the length required.

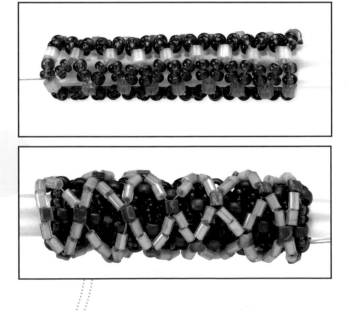

Five-bead netting makes a more open mesh than three-bead netting and, as a result, has more stretch. The strong contrast between the shared and bridge beads gives the rope an attractive spotty appearance.

Make **two ropes**, one with seed beads and the other with short bugles or more bridge beads to make a slightly larger tube with a more open mesh. Feed the thread tail through and pull one tube inside the other.

JOINING ROPES INTO RINGS

All the tubular stitches can be joined into a ring to make a chunky 'chain' link or to create a bracelet. For a professional finish, the stitch should continue around without any break in the pattern.

1. Make the beading tube the required length, leaving it a little short (one or two rounds of beads) to allow for extra beads added as you join the ends. Bring the ends together and look where you will need to add more beads; you may need to carry round to get to the next shared bead, ready to link into the other end.

2. Pick up two bridge beads and go through the next shared bead at the other end of the tube. Pick up another two bridge beads and go through the next shared bead on the first side of the tube. Carry round, filling in the bridge beads and then sew in the ends.

*Netting is one of the softest of the tubular bead stitches and wider versions need to be supported in order to make a piece of jewellery. This is often achieved by working a tube within a tube but with this design the netting is also supported by a length of satin rope. The pretty, variegated rope is a similar shade to the netting tube and makes it cylindrical. A contrast piece of tubular netting adds a finishing touch. See the Projects chapter for step-by-step instructions to make the **Net and Rope Bracelet**.*

Right-Angle Weave

Right-angle weave can be worked with small beads in a close weave to make bands of beading for cuff-style bracelets or as a loose, lacy mesh for a bib-style necklace. It is based on a basic four-bead unit, with each bead at right-angles to the next.

FLAT RIGHT-ANGLE WEAVE

Although you can work in the round to create a tube with right-angle weave, it is much easier to create a flat piece of beading the length and width required and then sew the long edges together to make a tube.

1. Pick up four beads and tie in a circle with a reef knot, leaving a long tail. Pass the needle through three beads so that the thread emerges at the opposite side to the tail. Pick up three beads and pass the needle back through the top bead, taking the needle through the next two beads in a clockwise direction to the next top bead.

2. Pick up three beads, pass the needle through the top bead then pass the needle through the beads in an anticlockwise direction to exit the next top bead again. Continue adding beads, alternating from clockwise to anticlockwise, making sure you exit from the top bead each time.

3. Take the needle round to come out from the bottom of a side bead in the top circle. Pick up three beads and pass the needle through the side bead again from top to bottom and then through the bottom bead.

4. From then on, as you use the beads already on the panel to create each circle, add only two beads each time down to the bottom of the chain. Alternate between clockwise and anticlockwise, taking the thread 'round the houses' to come out of the bottom bead each time.

TUBULAR RIGHT-ANGLE WEAVE

You can make either the three-sided tube shown here or one with four sides – simply work three columns of right-angle weave rather than two then join the sides together with the fourth side.

1. To form a three-sided tube, work two columns of right-angle weave as shown above. Bring the thread out at the bottom of a side bead. Pick up one bead, pass the needle from bottom to top through the side bead at the other edge and then pick up another bead. Go right round through the beads again and out at the bottom bead.

2. Continue joining the two edges together to create the tube, adding only one bead at the bottom of the circle each time until the tube is complete. Remember you will alternate between clockwise and anticlockwise as you work down the length. Sew in the thread ends securely.

EMBELLISHING

Right-angle weave can be stabilized and embellished with a diagonal stitch across each square unit. You can add one or more beads, depending on the size of the base unit.

• Bring the needle through a bottom bead of one column and pick up four or five seed beads. Pass the needle through the top bead in the opposite direction so that the beads lie diagonally across the right-angle weave.

• Continue until the rope is covered with extra beads. Go back in the other direction to form crosses (see the hugs and kisses technique).

ADDING CORNER BEADS

Right-angle weave is basically a four-sided unit with one bead each side. You can add corner beads, either as you work or afterwards. This example keeps the square format with four size 6 beads and four size 11 seed beads in each unit.

• Begin with a large bead and then pick up alternate small and large beads to make the unit. Tie the beads in a circle and pass back through the beads to come out at the top large bead.

• Pick up beads for the next circle and take the needle back throught the beads. When adding the next column, remember to add a small bead between the two large beads that you are 'borrowing' from the adjacent units to complete the new unit, so that there are four small beads in total.

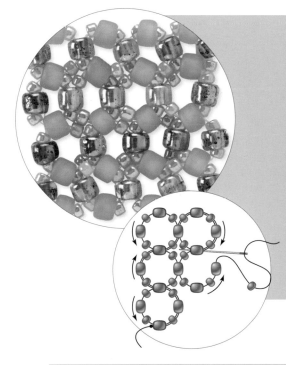

VARYING THE SHAPE

Units can be based on a rectangle, too, so that the basic 1 x 1 unit can be 1 x 2, 1 x 5 or any number of extra beads. The technique is the same – there are just more beads to go through in one direction. These longer units create a lacy fabric.

• Begin with the larger right-angle weave unit (1 x 5). Work enough units to get the first column the length required.

• Take the needle through the beads again until it emerges from the centre bead on one side. Add the first small unit and then add further small units until you are ready to link into the middle bead of the next large unit.

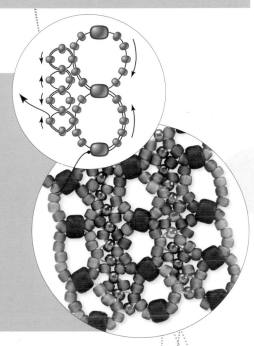

Flat Bead Weaving

There are many jewellery designs that are made by sewing thread through beads to create flat pieces of bead weaving, usually based on the right-angle weave technique. XILIONS (bicone) crystals are ideal for working these variations because of the way the beads fit together, but you can try other beads to make your own designs.

TRIANGLE WEAVE

In Japanese beadwork, triangle weave is used to create a motif called Hana-Ami, meaning flower stitch. You can work individual flowers for earrings or rings, join into a band for a bracelet or group together to make a bib-style necklace. Use a strong thread to make the shape quite rigid.

1. String six size 11 seed beads and tie them in a circle with a reef knot (see Tying Knots). Take the needle through the first bead again.

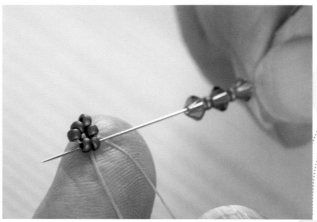

2. Pick up a (bicone) crystal, a seed bead, a crystal, a seed bead and another crystal and pass the needle through the first and second beads on the base circle again to make a triangle shape.

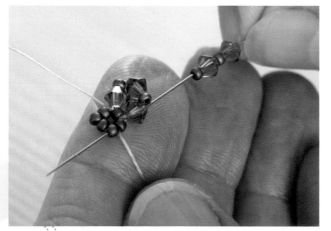

3. Pick up a crystal, a seed bead, a crystal and a seed bead. Pass the needle through the first crystal added last time and pass through the seed bead where the thread emerges and the next seed bead along.

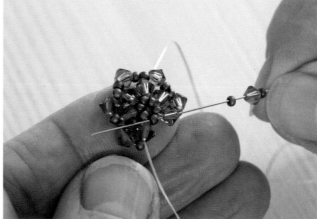

4. Continue around the centre circle of seed beads, repeating step 3 to add another three triangles. Take the needle through the adjacent seed bead and crystal, pick up a seed bead, a crystal and another seed bead and go back through the last crystal added and back out the adjacent crystal. Pull thread taut to complete the motif.

5. To create a band of motifs, take the needle through the top crystal on the last triangle formed. Pick up a seed bead, a crystal, a seed bead, a crystal and a seed bead. Pass the needle through the top crystal again, then through a seed bead, crystal and another seed bead to reach the centre of the new flower.

6. Pick up five more seed beads and go through the seed beads again to form a circle. Repeat from step 3 to finish. Continue to make as many Hana-Ami motifs as your require.

If you want to group the flower motifs, link through side beads rather than the opposite end beads used to create a band.

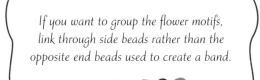

*By changing the size of beads, Hana-ami medallions can be made in a range of sizes and it is quite easy to join the different motifs as you work. For the best results, remember to grade the seed beads as well as the pearls and bicone crystals when making these pretty drop earrings. See the Projects chapter for step-by-step instructions for making the **Hana-ami Earrings**.*

HUGS AND KISSES

This variation uses the same techniques as right-angle weave but is worked with two needles rather than one. This example uses 4mm bicone crystals and size 11 seed beads.

$1.$ Thread a needle on both ends of a long thread. Pick up four crystals on one needle and drop down to the centre of the thread. Pass the other needle through the end crystal in the opposite direction and pull up to form a right-angle weave unit.

$2.$ Pick up one seed bead, a crystal, a seed bead, a crystal and a seed bead on each needle. Pick up a final crystal on one needle and pass the other needle through the crystal in the opposite direction.

$3.$ Pick up two crystals on one needle and one on the other. Pass that needle through the second crystal on the other side in the opposite direction. Repeat steps 2 and 3 until the band is the length you require.

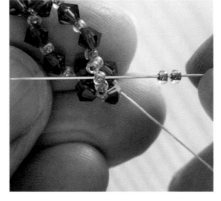

$4.$ Add the kisses embellishment on each four-bead unit: Pick up five seed beads on one needle and pass the needle in the opposite direction through the crystal at the other side of the unit.

$5.$ On the other needle, pick up two seed beads then pass the needle through the centre bead on the five beads just added. Pick up two more seed beads and pass the needle in the opposite direction through the end crystal again.

$6.$ Pass the needles through the 'hugs' bit of the band and take the needles in opposite directions through the end crystal ready to add the next 'kiss'. Sew in the thread ends, securing with a half-hitch knot.

> For small beads it may be necessary to use size B thread and a size 13 needle as you will be passing the needle and thread through each bead several times.

Medallions

Medallions, or rosettes, are bead stitches worked in a flat, circular form. They can be used singly as an earring or focal point, joined in a row to make a bracelet or clustered together to make a bib-style necklace. Use a size B or D braided or multifilament thread.

CIRCULAR HERRINGBONE STITCH

An attractive stitch worked as a medallion as the gaps between the stacks in the last round form a star shape that can be emphasized by adding an extra bead to each point. You begin in the same way as circular peyote stitch and so it is easy to change from peyote stitch to herringbone.

1. Create the base circle and work the first three rounds in the same way as steps 1–3 for circular peyote stitch. At the end of the third round, 'step up' through one blue and one grey bead ready to begin the herringbone stitch.

2. Pick up two beads and go back down through the next bead. Continue adding two beads to each pair of beads you added in the last round. At the end of the round you need to 'step up' through the nearest two beads on the first stack again.

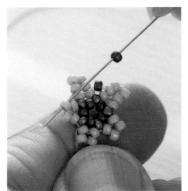

3. To increase on the next round, add a floating bead between each stack: *add two beads of herringbone stitch on the first stack and then pick up one bead and go into the next bead as usual. Repeat from *to the end of the round.

4. Step up again, work the first herringbone stitch, then add two floating beads before the next herringbone stitch. Continue adding two beads between each stack.

5. On the next round work herringbone into every two beads. On the next round pick up one bead between the stacks, then two beads in the next round before working herringbone stitch into the pairs of beads again. Repeat these three rounds until the circle is the size you want.

*To create a decorative finish to the **circular herringbone stitch** border on this ring, three tiny gold charlottes were added instead of the usual two beads on each stack.*

CIRCULAR BRICK STITCH

Circular brick stitch, often worked around a large central bead, is worked in the same way as regular brick stitch, with a 'step up' technique at the end of each round. To keep the flat shape you need to increase the number of beads or use progressively larger beads in each round.

 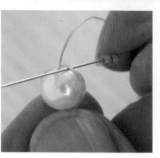  

1. Choose a large round or disc-shaped bead. Thread a needle with long thread and pick up the large bead. Drop down to about 15cm (6in) from the tail. Pass the needle back through the bead twice so that there is a thread on both sides.

2. Pick up two seed beads and pass the needle under the thread loop on one side of the large bead. Take the needle back through the second bead added and pull the thread taut.

3. Pick up another seed bead, pass the thread under the loop and back through the bead just added. Continue around the bead adding one bead at a time. Loop the thread through the first and last beads at the end of the round so that the thread finishes coming out of the first bead again.

4. Repeat from step 2 to begin the next round. If you are using the same size of beads you will need to add more beads to keep the piece flat. To increase, work two stitches into the same loop occasionally. Add as many beads as you need to keep the same spacing of beads in each round.

CIRCULAR PEYOTE STITCH

This technique creates a flat disc that can be embellished quite easily by increasing the beads added to make a frilled edge. To keep the medallion flat, work alternate rounds adding one or two beads each stitch. Alternatively, increase the bead size in each round.

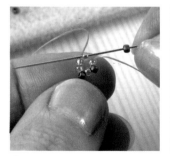 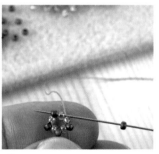  

1. Pick up five beads and pass the needle through the first two beads again to make a circle. For the second round add a bead between each bead in the base circle.

2. 'Step up' by passing the needle through the last bead of the base circle and the first bead added in the second round again.

3. Pick up two beads between each bead added in the last round. 'Step up' by passing the needle through the last bead in the previous round and one of the first two beads added this time, ready for the next round.

4. Add one bead between every bead in the previous round then, after stepping up, two beads between each of these beads in the following round. Repeat adding either one or two beads in each round, depending on the gap between the 'up' beads in the previous round, to keep the medallion flat.

Bezels

A bezel, worked in circular peyote stitch, is a rim of tiny seed beads that goes just over the edge of a large stone or cabochon. Bezels can be used to make rings, brooches and other pieces of jewellery. There is no decreasing but using progressively smaller beads allows the beadwork to curve in to enclose the cabochon and grip it securely.

1. String an even number of beads (eg size 11 hexagonal beads) to surround the cabochon, tie in a circle and pass the needle through a few beads to hide the knot, leaving a long tail. These beads form the first two rounds of circular peyote stitch.

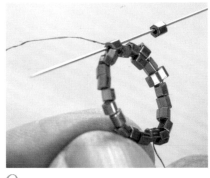

2. Pick up a bead on the needle, miss a bead on the circle and pass the needle through the next bead along. Continue adding beads one at a time by missing a bead and passing the needle through the next bead along.

3. At the end of the round take the needle through the first bead added again to 'step up' ready to begin the next round. The beadwork will now have the distinctive zigzag edge of peyote stitch with 'up' and 'down' beads.

4. Change to size 11 seed beads and continue adding between the 'up' beads from the previous round. Remember to step up through the first bead added in each subsequent round.

5. Add a round of size 15 cylinder beads and pull up tight, then a final round with tiny beads (size 15 Czech charlottes) to make a smooth thin edge on the collar. Take the thread through to the beginning row again.

6. Insert the cabochon face down and repeat the peyote stitch from step 4 to create a second beaded collar that holds the cabochon securely, again finishing with tiny charlotte seed beads.

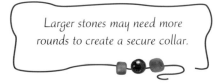

*Even **plain bezels** can look stunning; each crystal is surrounded by its own bezel and then they are all stitched together to create a fabulous brooch.*

Larger stones may need more rounds to create a secure collar.

ADDING A DECORATIVE COLLAR

Use circular herringbone stitch to add a flat collar to the bezel. The stacks in herringbone stitch are sturdy and stand out quite rigidly.

1. Bring the beading thread out between two beads in the middle of the three rows of cylinder beads on the edge of the bezel. Pick up two size 11 seed beads and go through the next hexagon along. Continue all the way round.

2. Step up through the first seed bead again. On the next round, work a herringbone stitch on each pair of beads, adding a floating bead between each stack. On the next round work a herringbone stitch on each pair of beads and add two floating beads between each stack.

3. Finally, work herringbone stitch all the way round into each pair of beads. To create the decorative pointed edge, add three tiny size 15 Czech charlottes or petites to the top of each stack.

ADDING A FRILLED COLLAR

For a different effect, force the collar to flare out and wave using peyote stitch between the herringbone stacks.

1. Work the bezel and begin to add the collar as shown in step 1, above, until you finish the first round of herringbone stitch with a single floating bead between each stack. Step up at the end of the round.

2. On the next round, step up and add the first two beads as herringbone stitch. Then work peyote stitch: pick up a seed bead and pass the needle through the floating bead. Pick up another seed bead and go through the first seed bead in the next stack ready to work another herringbone stitch.

3. Continue all the way round, alternating between herringbone and peyote stitch. On the next round you will work peyote stitch again between the stacks, adding three beads this time. Each subsequent round has more seed beads in the peyote stitch section, causing it to wave dramatically.

ADDING TEXTURE

You can further embellish the bezel by adding beads into the row of cylinder beads that are visible just inside the collar edge.

- Bring the thread out between two cylinder beads, pick up a small 3 or 4mm crystal and a tiny size 15 seed bead.
- Take the needle back through the crystal only and the next cylinder bead. Pull the thread taut, then add further crystals and seed bead stacks all the way round.

*Fancy stones with foil backing have a wonderful depth to their sparkle and when surrounded by a beaded bezel this effect is enhanced and it is like looking into a deep pool. Bezels can be left plain to create a simple ring or you can add a decorative collar. By increasing the beads in each round you can make the collar twist and wave to make a spectacular star effect. See the Projects chapter for step-by-step instructions for making the **Deep Pool Ring**.*

Netting

A versatile stitch, netting is a series of loops linked together to create a mesh, the size of which depends on the number of beads in each loop. The loops are connected by shared beads and the beads in between are called bridge beads. As the loops are connected into every second shared bead, there is a shared bead in the middle of each loop, too.

SINGLE THREAD VERTICAL NETTING

Working vertical netting with a single continuous thread between two end bars is one of the easiest netting techniques and can be used to create cuff-style bracelets or beautifully draped netting necklaces with one continuous thread. Use a size D strong beading thread to prevent fraying against the end bar.

1. Thread the cut ends of a very long double thread on to the needle. Take the needle through the first hole on your end bar and back through the loop to begin.

2. Pick up the required number of bridge beads (in this case 11) and a shared bead. Repeat to get the length required, making sure there is an even number of shared beads and ending with the bridge bead sequence.

3. Go through the end hole on the other part of the clasp and back through the last seed bead. Pick up 10 seed beads, a shared bead, then 11 seed beads. Miss a shared bead on the previous strand and go through the next shared bead. Repeat.

4. Repeat steps 2 and 3, going backwards and forwards until all the rings on the end bar are filled. Go back through a few beads, tie a half-hitch knot (see Tying Knots), repeat to make the thread really secure and trim the end.

MULTIPLE THREAD VERTICAL NETTINIG

This version is worked with pairs of threads attached to an end bar to make an attractive pendant or earrings.

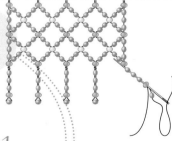

1. Fold long threads in half and attach one thread to each ring using a lark's head knot. Pick up all the beads for the sequence on the first strand.

2. For the second strand, pick up beads in sequence, remembering to omit every second shared bead and take the needle through the appropriate shared bead on the first strand. Once the netting is complete with beads added for the fringing, add a pivot bead to each fringe strand, go back through some of the beads and secure the thread with two half-hitches (see Tying Knots).

*Use **multiple thread netting** attached to sterling silver end bars to make a pair of elegant earrings.*

OGALALA LACE

This is a horizontal lace technique that is finished with a crinkly picot edge. The mesh size changes depending on the number of bridge beads added between the shared beads. You could also add more rows to create a deeper panel before working the picot edge.

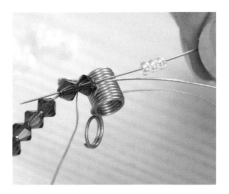

1. String an odd number of 4mm beads on a length of 0.018in bead stringing wire and attach a bead stopper spring at each end. Thread a size 10 or 12 beading needle with a 1.5m (1½yd) length of beading thread. Secure the thread into one of the bead stopper springs. Pass the needle through the first bead on the strand and pick up three size 11 seed beads. Pass the needle back through the same bead and the next one along.

2. Continue down the bead strand, picking up three seed beads and working backstitch through each 4mm bead. Pull the thread taut as you go and secure in the bead stopper spring at the other end.

3. Take the thread back through the last two seed beads added. Pick up two seed beads, a 4mm bead and another two seed beads. Take the needle through the middle bead in the loop of three seeds over the next 4mm bead.

> *Choose a 0.018in or even 0.012in bead stringing wire as you need to be able to pass a needle through the bead while it is on the bead stringing wire.*

4. Continue down the bead strand, adding the same sequence of five beads between the middle beads in each loop. Pull the thread taut as you go and add a half-hitch knot from time to time to prevent the thread loosening.

5. Add another row of loops using three seed beads, a 4mm bead and another three seed beads between the crystals. Now add the picot edge to create the lace effect. Pass the needle through the first of three seed beads added at the end of the bead strand. Pick up three seed beads and go though the last of these three seed beads.

6. Pick up another three seed beads and go through the first seed bead after the next 4mm bead. Pick up another three seed beads and go through the last seed bead before the next 4mm bead. Repeat this step until you get to the end. Sew in all the thread ends.

Bead Embroidery

Bead embroidery is one of the most tactile ways to work with beads and a wonderful way to create unusual and stylish jewellery. Single stitch, couching and backstitch are just some of ways to add beads to fabric and traditional embroidery stitches like chain stitch are also transformed with the addition of beads.

Getting Started

Most fabrics, from the sheerest georgette or organza to heavy denim and furnishing fabric, are suitable for bead embroidery but, before beginning, some planning is required as there is a tendency for the fabric to pucker, making it difficult to press out any creases.

TOOLS AND EQUIPMENT

Size 10 short needles with small eyes, such as sharps, are perfect for most beads but you may need a smaller size 13 for tiny beads and a larger needle for embroidery threads. Ordinary polyester sewing thread is quite suitable but you may prefer to use a stronger bead stitching thread in size B or D (see Choosing Thread). Small scissors with a fine sharp point are ideal for embroidery but for cutting fabric use dressmaker's shears.

TRANSFERRING DESIGNS

When working a set pattern or motif you will get better results if the design is transferred to the fabric before you begin.

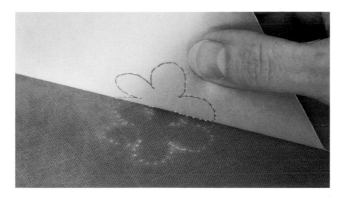

• PRICK AND POUNCE

A traditional method is 'prick and pounce' where a series of holes are pricked along the lines of the motif and then a small muslin bag of talcum powder is tapped over the template to transfer tiny dots of powder onto the surface of the fabric. You then lift up the template carefully and draw along the dotted lines with an embroidery marker.

• DIRECT TRACING

Tape the template and the fabric on to a work surface and draw along the lines with a vanishing embroidery marker. For dark or dense fabrics, tape the template and fabric to a light box or window to trace.

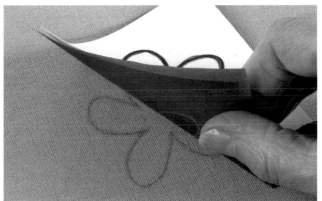

• TRANSFER PAPER

This coated paper is useful for transferring designs onto smooth fabric. Use a colour similar to the background fabric so that it is almost invisible behind the stitches. Lay the transfer paper coated side down on the fabric and position the template on top. Draw along the lines with a pencil or dressmaker's wheel.

BACKING FABRICS

Jewellery made from fabric generally needs to have a stiff lining or backing to create the shape. For bib-style or collar necklaces you can use heavy interfacing such as Vilene or pelmet backing but some backings, such as Lacy's Stiff Stuff, which can be dyed to match your beads, are specially made for bead embroidery. You can work the embroidery before backing or stitch through the stiff backing. For a slightly padded effect, layer thin quilting wadding between the fabric and the backing before embroidery.

EMBROIDERY HOOP

If you don't want to use a stiff backing, an embroidery hoop is useful for keeping fabric taut as you stitch. Unless the fabric is very thick, it is advisable to have a lining of some sort so you can sew in thread ends on the reverse side. Use a double layer of sheer fabrics to preserve the translucent effect and a lightweight lawn or calico for other fabrics.

Bind the inner hoop with cloth tape to prevent the fabric slipping.

BEGINNING AND FINISHING THREADS

It is important to secure threads carefully when working bead embroidery to prevent the beads falling off. When beginning, avoid a knot as it can unravel or pull through the fabric. Work with a double thread, even if the thread is apparently quite strong.

1. Take a tiny stitch through the reverse side of the backing fabric and then work a second tiny stitch on top to secure the thread. This is an ideal way to secure the thread at the end of the work too.

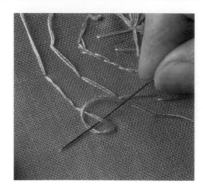

2. A quick method for finishing threads is the half-hitch knot. Make a loop of thread, take the needle under a previous stitch and then through the loop and pull through. Repeat the knot a couple of times for extra security.

SINGLE STITCH

Attach individual beads using single stitch. If the beads are spaced far apart, go through each bead a second time to secure the thread and prevent the beads pulling out.

1. Secure the thread on the reverse side (see Beginning and Finishing Threads) and bring out to the right side. Pick up a bead, drop it down to the fabric and hold the thread at the angle you wish to stitch.

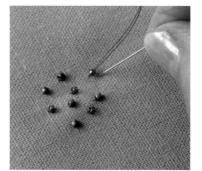

2. Insert the needle close to the end of the bead so that the needle is perpendicular to the fabric and take it through to the reverse side of fabric.

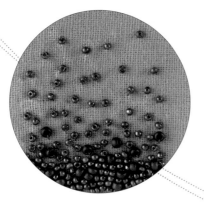

Work the stitches close together so that the fabric is almost completely covered in beads, or fill an area with a smattering of beads.

*Using embroidery thread, **make the stitches longer** so that thread is showing at each end.*

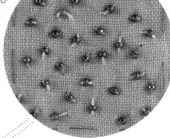

*Stitch in a **straight line** adding beads to disguise a seam or outline a motif or shape.*

STACKING SINGLE BEADS

Add larger beads or lots of small beads one above the other to add different textures. Bugle beads also add height and interest quickly. Graduate the sizes of the beads in each stack to create a smooth dome shape or work random lengths for a jaggy, textured effect. Whatever beads you choose use a small 'pivot' bead, usually a seed bead, at the top to secure the stack.

1. Bring the thread out where you want to add a large bead. Pick up the large bead and a small pivot bead. Take the needle back through the larger bead only and to the reverse side.

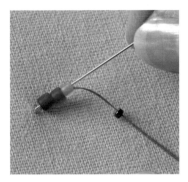

2. To create a stack, pick up several small beads and a small pivot bead, which can be the same or a contrast to the other beads. Miss the pivot bead and take the needle back through the other beads and through to the reverse side of the fabric.

Make a row of stacked beads along the edge of a piece of fabric to create a fringe.

*Jewellery can be complicated and use advanced techniques but sometimes the best designs are simple. All the beads in this exquisite bib-style necklace are added using single stitch. Although a little time consuming, adding the beads one at a time allows you to balance the colours and textures as you work. You can use any fine fabric as it will be completely covered in beads but silk dupion does give the finished piece a luxury feel. For step-by-step instructions to make the **Bead Encrusted Bib**, see the Projects chapter).*

Line Stitches

Professional bead embroiderers use a tambour hook for securing beads in lines or curves as it is quick and secure and easy to work on a commercial scale but for working at home you can use one of these techniques.

BACKSTITCH

This simple stitch is a secure way to add a few beads at a time and is a quick and accurate way to create short, curved lines. The needle goes back through the last couple of beads each time.

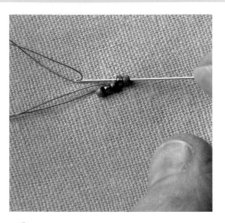

1. Secure the thread on the reverse side (see the technique for beginning and finishing threads) and bring it out to the right side. Pick up five beads and drop them down to the fabric. Hold the thread taut so that the beads are lying where you want them to be.

2. Take the needle down through the fabric at the end of the beads and back up between the third and fourth beads, as shown.

3. Pass the needle through the last two beads. Pick up the next five beads ready to work the next backstitch.

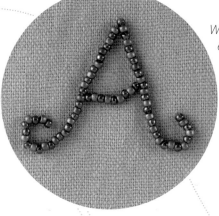

*When working **backstitch** bead embroidery, pick up fewer beads if you are working a tight curve and more beads for a straighter line.*

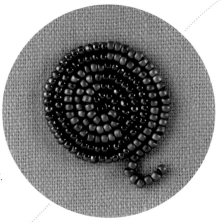

*If you are **filling an area** with backstitch it is important to space the lines out slightly so that the beads don't bunch up as you add more rows.*

COUCHING

Couching describes this stitch exactly as it is derived from the French verb 'se coucher', which means to lie down. Strings of beads are laid across the fabric and small stitches hold the line of beads in place. You can work short lengths of couching with a single thread or use two threads for longer lines.

SINGLE THREAD

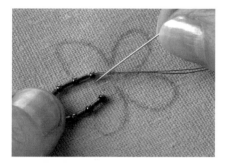

1. Secure two strands of thread on the reverse side and bring them out to the right side. Pick up enough beads to complete the line you want to create. Hold the thread taut and take the needle back through the fabric at the end of the beads, leaving a little slack for the couching stitches.

2. Bring the needle back through the fabric between the fourth and fifth beads from the end. Take the needle back through on the other side of the bead thread. Work back along the row of beads, taking a small stitch over the bead thread every four or five beads.

3. To create a curved line with a single thread use your thumb to hold the beads in the shape you want and then stitch over the beading thread one or two beads from the end to secure before working back along the line.

Work stitches between every two or three beads if the line is curved so that the shape is smooth.

*To create a **point** in beading, bring the needle out one or two beads back from the end of one line of beads and then add the next few beads to continue the new line.*

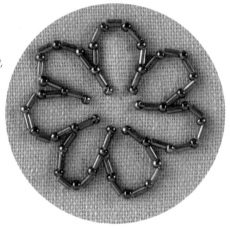

DOUBLE THREAD

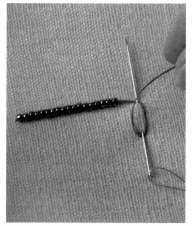

1. Secure a thread on the reverse side, bring it up where you want to begin and pick up enough beads to complete the line. Secure the thread beyond the end of the line by wrapping it around the needle or a pin.

2. Bring a second thread up between the fourth and fifth beads and take it back through on the other side of the bead thread. Work back along the row of beads taking a small stitch over the bead thread every four or five beads. Once the beads are couched, take the bead thread to the reverse side and sew in the thread ends.

Embroidery Stitches

Embroidery stitches take on a whole new look when beads are added. You can completely fill the stitch with beads or just add beads to a particular part of the stitch. Use an attractive thread such as stranded cotton, fine perlé cotton or silk thread as it is generally more visible than with ordinary bead embroidery.

CHAIN STITCH

Use chain stitch to make a double row of beads. You can either work ordinary chain stitch, where the threads emerge and go back through the same point, or widen the stitch to create two rows of beads with a gap in the middle.

1. Bring the needle up through the fabric and pick up four beads. Hold the beaded thread in a small loop then go back down through the fabric where the thread emerged.

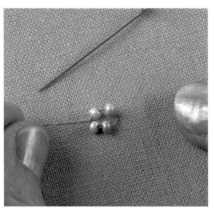

2. Bring the needle back up in the middle of the loop and pull the thread through to form the first chain stitch. To make an individual chain (lazy daisy stitch) catch the loop down with a tiny stitch.

3. To create a line of chain stitches, pick up another four beads and form the second chain stitch loop. Take the needle back down where the thread emerged. Repeat as required.

4. To work the wider stitch, bring the needle up through the fabric, add the beads and form a loop. Take the needle back through the fabric about 3–6mm (1/8–¼in) from where it emerged.

*Use a **variety of bead sizes** to create a richly textured line of beads. Vary the tones of the beads within one colour way to avoid making it too bitty.*

BUTTONHOLE STITCH

Buttonhole or blanket stitch is a versatile stitch for bead embroidery. Stitch in lines with beads along the top edge or work in a curve or circle to create spiky motifs. You can sew two pieces of fabric together, adding the beads so that they sit along the edge of the fabric or on the other leg of the stitch to make a border.

1. Bring the thread up through the fabric and pick up two beads. Work a vertical stitch about 3–6mm (⅛–¼in) further across. Pass the thread under the needle so that the beads are between the needle and where the thread first emerged.

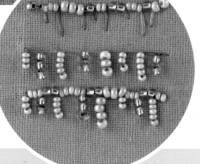

2. Pull the needle through to create the 'L' shaped stitch. Pick up two more beads and take a vertical stitch again. You could also leave the beads on the vertical leg of the stitch.

When sewing two layers together, use a stabbing motion so that the stitch is the same size on both sides.

*Add beads to the top bar, the lower bar or to both to create a **range of textures**, varying the length of the stitch to create a zigzag or wavy effect.*

FLY STITCH

Use fly stitch to create little loops of beads or add beads on the tail as well to create a 'Y' shaped stitch.

1. Bring the needle up through the fabric and pick up four beads. Hold the beaded thread in a small loop then go back down through the fabric about 3–6mm (⅛-¼in) from where it emerged.

2. Bring the needle back up in the middle of the loop and pull the thread taut to create a 'V' shape. You can either work a tiny stitch over the bead thread to hold it down or a longer stitch to create a tail.

***Vary the stitch** by adding beads to the tail only or add beads to both the 'V' and the tail. Work single stitches side by side to create a border.*

ATTACHING SEQUINS

There are several ways to attach sequins to fabric. You can sew the sequins individually or overlapping in a row. These techniques are also suitable for attaching washer-style beads.

1. Secure the thread on the reverse side. Position the sequin where you want it and bring the needle up through the middle of the sequin. Take the needle back down at the side. A second stitch secures the sequin and a third in a 'Y' shape will make it safe enough to launder.

2. To secure with a bead, position the sequin where you want it and bring the needle and thread up through the middle of the sequin. Pick up a seed bead and take the needle back down through the hole in the sequin only. You can make a tiny backstitch on the reverse side for added security before attaching the next sequin.

Sequins can be sewn individually or in straight or curved lines.

ATTACHING SEQUINS IN A ROW

1. Position the first sequin and take a stitch from the centre hole and over the right hand edge. Bring the needle and thread back through to the right side.

2. Position the next sequin so that it covers the last stitch. Bring the thread up through the hole in the second sequin and over the right hand edge. Repeat until the line is as long as required.

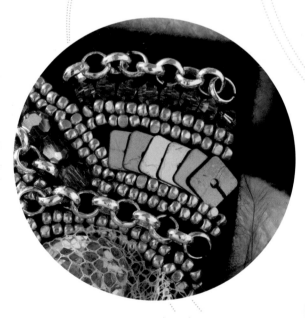

Sequins are very quick and easy to attach and can be used in so many decorative ways.

Three quite different fabrics come together in perfect harmony to create this exquisite brooch; felt is used as a non-fray base, silk organza to add interest and fine tulle netting to secure the larger crystals and add texture. Black feathers are added to highlight the two paler fabrics and the design embellished with sequins, charlotte seed beads, crystals and chain. You can add a brooch back or hang the brooch on a giant kilt pin. For step-by-step instructions for making the **Feather and Fabric Brooch** see the Projects chapter.

Finishing Techniques

To turn a piece of beaded fabric into something you can wear, you can sometimes simply attach it to a hair comb, Alice band or brooch back, but often you will need to stretch the fabric over a stiff backing or a blank piece of jewellery, such as a bangle.

GATHERING

Fabric can be gathered around the edges to draw in any excess fabric and hide the raw edges. This technique is ideal for round or oval shapes and light, thin fabrics; see Snipping and Notching (below) for heavier fabrics.

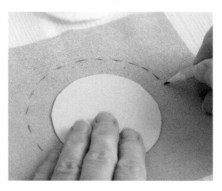

1. Cut a piece of stiff interfacing, to the exact shape and size of your jewellery design. Cut a piece of thin wadding the same size and lay on top; you can cut progressively smaller pieces of wadding for a higher, domed effect.

2. Position the embroidered fabric under the backing then mark and trim around the edge leaving a 6–12mm (¼–½in) border all round. Sew a line of running stitch around the fabric edge.

3. Reposition the bead embroidery around the backing then pull up the thread to gather the fabric. Sew a tiny backstitch to secure temporarily, check the beading is straight then even out the gathers and sew in the thread end.

STRETCHING

Use this technique for other shapes with convex and concave curves where gathering is unsuitable. Prepare the embroidered piece and the backing in the same way as for gathering (step 1 above).

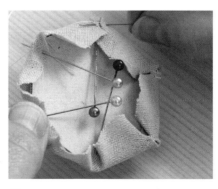

1. Position the embroidered fabric over the backing then trim around the edge leaving a 6–12mm (¼–½in) border. Cut across corners, leaving enough fabric to cover the edge of the backing.

2. Fold in the trimmed corners and then the flaps on each side. Pin or tack in position. Secure a strong thread to one edge of the fabric, take a tiny stitch on the flap on the opposite side.

3. Work backwards and forwards across the shape, then pull the thread taut. Check the positioning on the front and then stretch in the opposite direction. Pull the thread taut again, and sew in the thread end to secure.

FINISHING

Once the beaded fabric has been stretched to the correct shape you may want to cover the back as neatly as possible. You can use thin leather, felt or another fabric that doesn't fray, or back with the same fabric as used for the embroidery.

1. Cut a piece of fabric 6mm (¼in) larger all round than the stretched jewellery panel. Snip or notch (see belwo), then turn in the edges of the fabric and tack or press in position so that the shape is slightly smaller than the original.

2. Lay the prepared fabric over the back of the bead embroidery piece. Pin if necessary then work tiny oversewing stitches or invisible slipstitches around the edge, stretching the fabric slightly as you go.

3. Alternatively use this technique – ideal for gathered pieces. Cut felt or a similar non-fray fabric slightly smaller than the original template. Pin or tack in position, covering the raw edges. Use tiny over sewing stitches to attach as above.

4. Stitch brooch backs near the top of the bead embroidered panel so that it hangs correctly when worn. If you stitch the brooch back in the middle it will be top heavy and hang forwards.

COVERING A BANGLE

Recycle old bangles or use a ready-made blanks to create new jewellery. The fabric can be embroidered with beads before you stretch or, with care, afterwards.

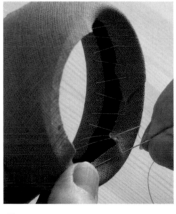

1. Cut a strip of fabric longer than the circumference of the bangle and about 1cm (½in) shorter than the measurement around the cross section. Stitch the back seam and ease over the bangle so the seam is on the inside. Sew raw edges together. Sew all the way round going back and forwards inside the bangle.

2. Cut a paper template to fit the inside surface of the bangle. Cut felt slightly narrower width-wise. Sew in position using tiny oversewing stitches and then butt the ends and stitch neatly. You can also use the same fabric, with the edge turned under, to cover the inside of the bangle.

SNIPPING AND NOTCHING

To make fabric jewellery flat and neat you need to reduce the bulk on the reverse side. You can trim across the corners but for curves you should snip or notch before stretching.

Snip into concave curves so that they open out as you fold the flap over. Cut little notches into convex curves so that the flap lies flat when you fold it over. The more curved the edge the greater the number of snips and notches.

Making Beads, Charms and Pendants

Although there is a multitude of ready-made beads, charms and pendants, it can still be difficult to find exactly what you need and you may want to try making some of these yourself. This chapter shows the variety of materials and some techniques that can be used to make unique pieces of fabulous jewellery.

Beaded Beads

Beaded beads can be made by covering larger beads with small beads using a variety of techniques, such as wrapping, or can be made entirely using sead beads and one or more of the bead stitches described in the previous chapter.

WRAPPED BEADS

Any large round or oval bead can be covered with smaller beads to create a wrapped bead. Pressed cotton balls are ideal for wrapping because they can be painted or dyed to match the smaller beads and they are very light to keep the weight of the finished bead down.

1. Tie a long thread through the hole in the bead or pressed cotton ball. Pick up sufficient beads to reach round from one hole to the other. Take the needle back through the hole.

2. Keep adding rows of beads all the way round. Go back, filling in the gaps with shorter bead rows until the bead is completely covered. Tie the thread ends together.

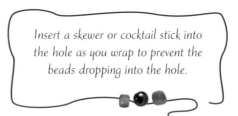

Insert a skewer or cocktail stick into the hole as you wrap to prevent the beads dropping into the hole.

NETTING BEADS

Large beads can be covered using any of the circular bead stitches in chapter 7 but one of the easiest techniques to use is netting. To find out more about working netting with shared and bridge beads see the Tubular Netting technique. Whether you use netting or one of the other stitches, make sure you increase or decrease so that the beading follows the shape of the bead.

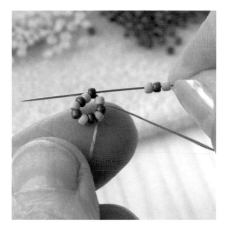

1. Pick up ten beads in alternating colours and tie in a circle. Pass the needle through the beads, coming out after a dark (shared) bead. Pick up a light (bridge) bead, a shared bead and a bridge bead. Take the needle through the next shared bead in the base circle.

2. Repeat all the way round to create a five-pointed star. 'Step up' by taking the needle through the first three beads on the first loop again, ready to begin on the next round of loops.

3. Pick up two bridge beads, a shared bead and two bridge beads. Pass the needle through the shared bead in the next loop. Repeat all the way round. Step up ready to begin the next round.

4. Continue adding more beads in each round until you reach the middle of the bead, then reduce the number of beads so the netting follows the shape of the bead. Finish this end to match the other end, adding a single seed bead between the bridge beads in the last round. Pull up tight and sew in the ends.

*A mix of Swarovski crystals and sparkly seed beads make a stunning **beaded bead** for a bag charm or key ring.*

BEAD STITCHED BEADS

Any of the tubular bead stitches described in Bead Stitches, chapter 7, can be turned into a beaded bead. Simply make a small tube with only six or seven beads in the base circle and add texture by varying the type of beads. Use beads with a large hole such as cylinders or Toho seed beads for the tubes as the needle and thread have to go through the bead holes several times.

MAKING THE BASE TUBE

PEYOTE STITCH:
Pick up seven beads and work odd-count peyote stitch, following the technique in Bead Stitches, to make a short tube.

HERRINGBONE STITCH:
Make a six-bead single ladder stitch base, work five rows of herringbone stitch and finish with a row of ladder stitch to match the other end.

BRICK STITCH:
Make a six-bead ladder stitch base and follow the instructions for brick stitch in Bead Stitches, but don't increase the beads in the following five or six rounds and you'll create a short tube.

LOOPS
You can make short or long loops to cover the tube surface. Work over one bead, several or the whole length. The loops can be worked vertically or horizontally or even diagonally for different effects.

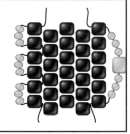

STACKS
Stacks are made in the same way as a short fringe where you take the needle through a pivot bead and back through one or more beads to create a short stack of beads. Experiment with beads and bugles.

FRILLS
Use **three-bead netting** to create a frill effect on a plain tube. For a fuller effect add more beads on the second round.

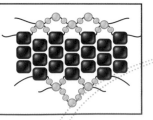

For short loops, add one or more slightly larger beads to span the same number of beads on the base tube, or simply add an extra bead for the loop.

Adding short bugles with a seed bead at the top makes a spiky texture

Using the netting technique opposite, work two rows of netting around the middle of the tube for a different shape.

To create a cotton reel shape, work two rows of netting at each end of the tube: first round in three bead netting and then five in the second round.

Satin seed beads held in place with a smaller pivot bead, create a bubbly texture on the surface of the tube.

Long loops can be worked vertically, horizontally or diagonally for interesting effects

Embellished beaded beads
look fabulous when strung
together with round glass
beads to make a simple
memory wire bracelet.

Paper

Beads can be made from all sorts of paper in a variety of techniques. The most popular technique is rolling, often associated with children's bead making, but these easy to make beads, can look quite spectacular if you embellish with paints or inks before varnishing.

ROLLING

All sorts of paper can be rolled into beads as long as it is fairly thin but strong so that it doesn't tear. The coloured pages of magazines allow you to create a wide range of different colours and junk mail is good, too, but look for larger sheets so that there are not too many joins. You can make thin beads with one strip of paper, and chunkier beads if you roll two or three strips together.

1. Cut graduated strips about 28cm (11in) long depending on the style of bead you want to make (see chart below). Mark 2cm (¾in) at one end of the magazine page and mark the mid point of 2cm (¾in) at the other end. Draw lines to make a triangle shape and cut out.

2. Begin to roll the strip from the widest end. Roll around a cocktail stick or similar and apply a drop of glue to secure. Leave a moment to dry, then apply a thin line of glue down the middle of the strip and roll up, keeping the strip central.

3. You can use the beads as they are or decorate them with oil paint sticks, spray inks or other mediums, then coat with matt or gloss varnish.

4. When making fatter beads, tuck the next strip under just as you get to the end and leave to dry again. Apply more glue down the next strip and roll up. Join on subsequent strips in the same way and roll up completely.

	First strip	Second strip	Third strip
2cm thin bead	2cm–1mm (¾–¹⁄₃₂in)		
1cm round bead	1cm–5mm (½–¼in)	5mm–1mm (¼–¹⁄₃₂in)	
2cm oval bead	2–1.5cm (¾–⅝in)	1.5–1cm (⅝–½in)	1cm–5mm (½–¼in)

If the final strip comes to a fine point you will make a Bicone shape of bead, a wider end to the last strip creates a barrel shape; a strip like a two-pointed flag will make a bead shape like a diabolo.

DÉCOUPAGE

You can change the look of a plain bead completely by covering in thin patterned or solid coloured paper using a découpage technique. Tissue paper and napkins can be used or try décopatch, which is a paper made specially for covering surfaces (see Suppliers). Once covered, you can decorate your beads with inks or paints.

1. Tear the tissue paper up into tiny pieces; it helps to scrunch the paper first. Apply a little glue in a thin layer to the bead. Pick up a piece of paper with the brush and apply to the surface.

2. Brush over the paper to smooth it down and then apply more pieces one at a time. Apply more glue as required. Once the bead is covered completely, dab all over with the brush and leave to dry.

For spotty beads, cover the bead completely in a solid colour the same background as the spots, then tear around a few spots and apply these pieces of paper on to the solid colour.

*The rolled and découpage beads were made from similar **coloured papers** but coordinated even more by applying specks of oil-based artists sticks to all the beads. They look quite fabulous strung with 'real' beads.*

Fabric and Fibres

You can manipulate fabric and fibre in any way you want to make bead shapes, but there are particular techniques that will get you started. If you wish, you can apply glue or some other stiffener to fabric to make hard beads. Beads can be embellished with seed beads, embroidery and other fibres.

WRAPPING

Fabric can be rolled into a bead shape in a similar way to making paper beads, or you can wrap a plain bead with thin strips of fabric and then wrap with thread or fibres to secure the fabric, further shape the bead and embellish it. Fabric can also be wrapped around items like thin straws or wooden rings to make different shapes.

1. Apply a small strip of double-sided tape around the bead and then thread on to a large needle or skewer to make it easier to hold as you wrap. Cut thin strips of fabric and wrap around the bead. Continue to wrap further strips around it, keeping the shape round and smooth.

2. Wrap fibres or thread around the bead, changing directions several times to cover the bead evenly. Use two or three different colours or textures. Sew in ends through the fabric to secure. Paint with a clear drying PVA glue and leave to dry before removing the needle.

3. Doughnut shaped beads, in particular inexpensive wooden rings, can be embellished with thin strips of fabric and then wrapped with thread to secure in the same way as the round beads.

SUFFOLK PUFFS

These pretty, gathered, circular motifs could be used in the same way as medallions to make bib-style necklaces and other jewellery. The puffs can be made from any fairly thin fabric and can be left plain or embellished further with beads and fibres.

1. Cut a circle of fabric about twice the size of the finished puff. Thread a needle with thread and knot the end. Folding over a small turning as you go, sew a row of running stitches around the edge.

2. Once you sew all the way round, pull the thread to draw the fabric in and create a gathered puff. Sew the thread end in securely. Add beads to embellish if required.

FELT BEADS

There are lots of different ways to make felt beads but this technique is a quick way to make several beads in a similar size. Use Merino felting fibres for a smooth finish to your beads. Once the beads are made you can embellish them with embroidery or beads. Push a large needle through the felt to make a hole.

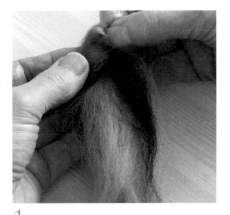 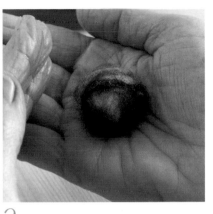 

1. Tease out pieces of felt fibre and layer, overlapping to make a small bundle. Wet your hands and then begin to roll the felt fibres in from one end. Fold in the edges as you go to make a tight little ball to start. Continue rolling up, changing direction from time to time to keep the round shape. Roll ends over the felt fibre ball smoothly.

2. Wet your hands again and apply a little glycerine or olive oil soap this time. Roll in circular movements between the palms of your hand to make the bead shape. You can make oval or cylinder shapes, too, depending on the way you roll the fibres.

3. Stop rolling when the bead is no longer fuzzy. Rinse in cold water and put to one side to dry. Repeat steps 1–3 to make more beads. Use the same amount of felt fibre to create beads the same size.

Once the felt beads are dry you can stitch seed beads all over the surface, one at a time.

*Embellish **Suffolk puffs** with crystals and metallic threads to create a pretty embellishment for a tiara or hairband. Make wrapped and felted beads with similar colours and fibres and secure between the puffs with fine wire.*

Polymer Clay

Polymer clay can be shaped by hand, modelled, cut out or shaped with bead rollers and then baked to harden. There are lots of simple techniques that can be used to make and decorate beads, pendants and components for jewellery.

ADDING TEXTURE

Before using the clay, condition it by rolling between the palms of your hands so that it is soft enough to shape easily. Roll directly onto a ceramic tile and you don't need to move it to bake.

1. Roll a piece of polymer clay about 6mm (¼in) thick, directly onto a ceramic tile. Smear Badger Balm over a rubber stamp. Press into the clay keeping the stamp level and lift off carefully.

2. Use a knitting needle or skewer to make dots or lines on the surface as additional texture. To create a wonderful sheen, brush the surface with two or three different shades of mica powder to highlight the raised surface.

3. Cut into shape with a knife or a shape cutter. Carefully lift away any excess clay. Make a hole with a skewer or straw and bake in the oven according to the manufacturer's instructions. You can place the tile in the refrigerator for several hours to firm up before you lift the pieces off.

MAKING BEADS

It is fun to roll clay between your hands to make balls or on a flat surface to make sausages and then experiment with shaping, texturing and mixing colours. These Pandora-style beads look like the real thing!

1. Roll a small quantity of two or three different colours of clay into thin sausages all the same length. Twist the sausages together and then curl up in your hand. Roll the clay round between the palms of your hand to make a marbled effect.

2. Roll bead-size pieces into a ball and flatten slightly. Place in the refrigerator for several hours. Make a hole with a needle, then go through with a skewer, working up to a 5mm knitting needle, or to match the size of your grommet.

3. Insert a 5mm grommet into the hole at each side of the bead. Bake in the oven according to the manufacturer's instructions. The clay shrinks very slightly to secure the grommets but these can also be glued in place once the bead has cooled.

MILLEFIORI

Originally used in Venetian glassware, Millefiori (a thousand flowers) is easy to work in polymer clay. Choose a dark contrast colour for step 2 so that there is clear definition in later stages. You can cut segments and make beads at any stage of the process.

1. Condition two balls of ivory clay and then roll a sausage of clay by hand until it is about 1cm (½in) thick. Roll out a single ball of black clay using a small rolling pin until it is about 1mm (⅟₁₆in) thick. Trim one long edge straight, then roll the sausage up inside to cover. Trim any excess.

2. Roll the sausage again by hand until it is about 15cm (6in) long. Try to keep it the same diameter all the way along.

3. Cut into four sections and bundle together with the cut surfaces level at one end. Roll a ball of a second colour very thin. Trim one short end and one long side straight and use to cover the four sausages again.

4. Repeat step 2 to make a thinner sausage, then cover the new sausage shape with a third colour. Roll this thin and cut into four. Layer as before.

Cut straight or diagonal slices through the millefiori to create beads or pendants.

*Make a selection of Pandora beads from **three colours of clay**, some solid colours and some marbled, and then coat with mica powder before baking.*

Metal Clay

Metal clay has fine particles of metal mixed in an organic base with water. It can be rolled, moulded and shaped like ordinary clay and then, once dry, it is fired with a gas (cook's) torch until it transforms into fine silver. Then you can drill, file and hammer it, just like real silver. These basic techniques will get you started.

ROLLING AND TEXTURING

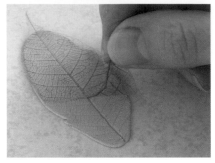

1. Smear Badger Balm on a ceramic tile or work on a Teflon sheet to prevent the metal clay sticking and roll out to 1.5mm (⅛in). You can use plastic spacer strips or pile three or four playing cards one on top of the other on either side of the clay instead.

2. Texture the clay with pointed tools, a knife or rubber stamp to create a pattern. Alternatively, lay a skeleton leaf on top of the clay and roll gently with the rolling pin. Peel off carefully and smooth any ragged edges with your finger.

3. Cut the textured clay to size using a sharp blade or a cutter. Peel away the excess, wrap closely in plastic wrapping and return to airtight packaging. Leave to dry overnight, then fire and finish as for the shell below.

> *Smear Badger Balm or olive oil on to rubber stamps or skeleton leaves before pressing into the clay.*

MAKING A MOULD

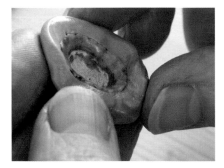

1. Mix equal quantities of each colour of the resin moulding compounds until the two are completely merged.

2. Smear the item you'd like to mould with Badger Balm and press into the moulding compound. Try to keep the material a similar thickness all round and bring it up level with the top of the item, in this case a shell.

3. Leave the mould for about five minutes to firm up and then remove the shell. Trim the mould if necessary with a sharp craft knife and smear the inside surface with Badger Balm.

4. Roll out a thin sheet of metal clay (see step 1 above). Press the clay into the mould. Use a large ball-end tool or your finger to press the clay down. Push the clay against the mould, easing away any excess with your thumb. Wrap any scraps and package up. Ease out the clay shape and leave to dry overnight.

5. Lay the clay shape on a heat mat. Light the gas torch and wave over the clay until it glows red hot. Keep at that temperature for a few moments until you see the clay transforming. Stop before the silver melts or you will lose the detail. Leave to cool or plunge into a dish of water to speed up the process.

6. File away any rough edges. Scrub the silver with a fine wire brush to bring out a satin finish on the silver. Untextured silver can also be burnished with a smooth metal tool to create a beautiful polished surface.

*Drill holes at the top of **silver shell beads** and hang with crystal bead dangles to make a pretty charm bracelet.*

Plastic

Shrink plastic and friendly plastic both have fairly low melting points and can be shaped and cut to make a variety of beads, pendants or charms. Both plastics can be melted or shrunk using a craft heat gun and can be textured with rubber stamps then coloured with ink-pads, pens, alcohol inks and other paper-crafting techniques.

SHRINK PLASTIC

Shrink plastic is available in a range of colours as well as clear, translucent, frosted and black. The plastic can be rolled while still warm to create beads, or twisted and shaped to make charms.

1. Diecut a 7cm (2¾in) circle from frosted shrink plastic (plastic without frosting needs to be lightly sanded on one side first) and punch a 5cm (2in) circle from the centre. Punch a 1cm (½in) hole at one side of the circle.

2. Apply purple pigment ink to a scroll pattern stamp. Stamp the reverse, frosted, side of the shrink plastic circle. Dab purple ink on the frosted side of the ring using a small piece of sponge until it is evenly covered.

3. You can punch holes into the plastic at this stage; remember that the hole size will shrink by 50%. Lay one of the shrink plastic pieces on a heat resistant surface and heat with a heat gun. The plastic will curl but eventually unfurls and lays flat. Repeat to shrink the second piece.

FRIENDLY PLASTIC

Friendly Plastic is a non-toxic material that is easy to use without any special tools. Here's a guide to making pendants and connectors.

1. Smear a ceramic tile with petroleum jelly to prevent the plastic sticking. To soften, lay the plastic on the tile and heat with a craft heat gun until you can make a deep impression with your fingernail.

2. To join two pieces of plastic to make a wider strip, trim the bevelled edge off one edge of each piece and lay butted together on the ceramic tile. Heat the plastic gently with the craft heat tool and then leave to cool.

3. Heat the plastic until soft. Stamp with ink or smear the stamp with petroleum jelly before pressing into the plastic. Lift off once completely cool.

4. Friendly Plastic can be coloured with alcohol inks. Dilute the ink with an equal quantity of blending solution and then paint any raised areas. Once this layer is dry you can paint a second layer and use undiluted ink for more depth of colour.

5. You need to heat the plastic again before cutting. Take care not to overheat or the image you have stamped will flatten. Cut with a sharp kitchen knife or cutters. Avoid twisting the cutter as the edges of softened friendly plastic will become distorted.

6. Soften the plastic with a heat gun again, then use a hole punch or even a straw in the correct size to punch a hole for hanging. Always leave to cool completely before lifting off the tile.

*Using two contrasting colours of **friendly plastic** adds an interesting two-tone effect to this pretty pendant.*

*A little wax cotton, tied and finished with tiny end caps is all that is needed to turn these pretty stamped and coloured circles made from **shrink plastic** into a pair of earrings.*

Bead Projects

Jewellery making is a tremendously varied craft with a phenomenal range of beads and materials that can be used to create the designs brought together in this chapter. This variety means that each of the projects can be created exactly as shown, in another colour scheme or with quite different beads to make a unique design – the choice is yours. The projects come from different chapters in the book to showcase the various techniques that can be used to create jewellery. Follow the illustrated step-by-step instructions here and, if you need further guidance, refer back to the chapter that features that particular design.

Juicy Pearls

Wrapped loop links are much more prominent in a necklace design than plain loops but here the wrapped loop is essential as brass wire isn't hard enough to support the weight of these large glass pearls with a plain loop. Arrange the pearls carefully so that no two of the same colour are opposite one another when worn.

YOU WILL NEED:

• Glass pearls 15mm, seven ivory, one gold, one pinky/red, one dark green
• Glass pearls 8mm, six burnt pink, six burnt orange
• Glass pearls 7mm, 36 lime green
• Brass wire, 0.6mm (24 swg)
• Brass or antique copper headpins, 21
• Snipe- (chain-) nose pliers

1. Make 12 plain loop bead dangles with the 8mm pearls (see the Plain Loop technique). Make nine plain loop bead dangles with the 7mm lime green pearls.

2. Cut a 10cm (4in) length of brass wire. Make a wrapped loop (see the wrapped loop technique) at one end of the first length. Pick up a 15mm dark green pearl on the wire and make a wrapped loop at the other end.

3. Attach the bead dangles to the loop at one end of the dark green pearl, opening and closing the loops with snipe-nose pliers.

4. Make a wrapped loop on a 9cm (3½in) length of brass wire. Pick up a 7mm lime green pearl and then pre-form the loop at the other end. Link into the free loop on the dark green pearl and finish the wrapped loop. Add a 15mm ivory pearl with another wrapped link. This forms the dangle at the bottom of the necklace.

5. Continue adding wrapped bead links to make the main necklace: lime green, ivory, lime green then burnt pink. Add a wrapped loop to the burnt pink. Pick up two burnt orange, two deep pink and three lime dangles on the wire. Make a wrapped loop at the other end.

6. Continue adding wrapped loop links: ivory, lime, ivory and then 22 lime wrapped bead links. Work down the other side of the necklace adding an ivory, lime and ivory pearl. Create a wrapped loop again through the last ivory pearl, pick up the remaining bead dangles and then make a wrapped loop at the end again.

7. To finish the necklace, add ivory, lime, gold and lime pearls. Attach the last lime pearl into the top loop of the ivory pearl added in step 4 above.

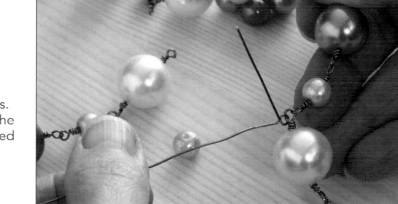

Crystal Statement Ring

This style of ring is usually beyond the capabilities of most of us as it generally requires soldering to secure the different settings together. The settings that fit SWAROVSKI ELEMENTS Fancy Stones have holes in the side, which allows the same effect to be produced without the need for specialist tools and skills.

YOU WILL NEED:

• SWAROVSKI ELEMENTS

– XILION Navette 4228, 15 x 7mm, one emerald (F205), one fuschia (F502)

– XILION Chaton, round stone 1028, 8mm, one topaz (F 203), one indicolite (F 379), 3 x 5.5mm crystal AB (F 001AB)

– Drop Fancy Stone 4300, 10 x 6mm, one montana (F 207), one amethyst (F 204)

• Silver-plated settings: two navette 15 x 7mm, two round stone 8mm, three round stone 5.5mm, two drop 10 x 6mm

• Silver-plated wire, 0.4mm (27swg)

• Silver-plated ring base

• Epoxy resin glue

1. Insert each of the stones into its setting so that it is lying level. Hold the stone and carefully flatten each of the lugs in turn with the side of a pair of pliers or similar tool.

2. Arrange the set stones as shown in the photograph of the finished ring. Cut a 40cm (16in) length of 0.4mm silver-plated wire and bend gently in half. Thread the ends through the holes in the pink navette stone setting and pull through so that the wires are of equal length.

3. Pick up the montana drop stone and feed the two wires through that setting too. Follow the diagram to make sure that you have the stone facing in the right direction.

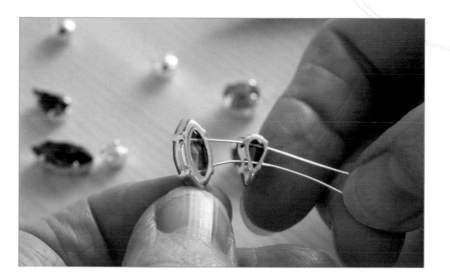

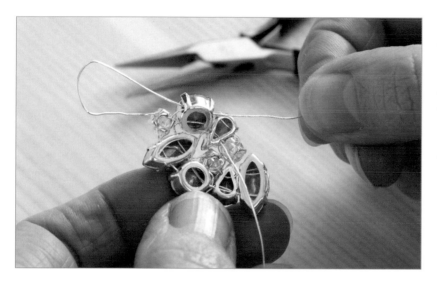

4. Continue to add stones, following the diagram. You will add a table diamond on one wire and a round stone on another, then take both wires through the emerald navette. Add the remaining stones as shown. Pull up the wires as tight as possible taking care not to snap them.

5. You need to pass the wire around the settings in a slightly different direction to stabilise the arrangement. Take the wires into the centre on the reverse side, twist the ends together, trim and tuck down flat.

6. Spread a thin layer of quick setting, clear epoxy resin glue on the wires on any unstable stones on the reverse side of the arrangement. Leave to dry. Attach a ring base to the underside of the setting using a little epoxy resin glue. Hold until it has set, making sure the jewels are facing in the right direction relative to the ring base.

Silky Pearl Bracelet

Simple freshwater pearls strung on silk thread can be worn for almost any occasion and always look fabulous. The knots are tied to prevent the pearls from rubbing together and losing their sheen but they also improve the drape considerably. This technique is neat, professional and secure enough to be finished without glue.

YOU WILL NEED:

- Fresh water pearls, 7 x 8mm, approx. 21
- Silk cord no 5 (0.65mm)
- Jump rings, soldered and silver-plated, two
- Sterling silver fastening
- Gimp, 2cm (1in)

Use silk cord with an integral needle and check that two thicknesses of thread will fit through the bead.

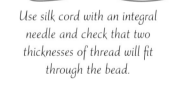

1. Unravel the cord, tie a loose knot on the end, then thread on three pearls and a 1cm (½in) piece of gimp. String on a soldered ring or jump ring. Take the needle back down through the first pearl.

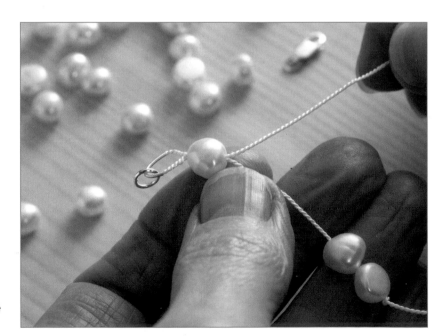

2. Tie a half-hitch (see Tying Knots) over the tail of the silk cord and pull both cords to move knot next to the pearl. Repeat to add a knot after the second and third pearls.

$3.$ String on a fourth pearl leaving the tail sticking out to one side. Tie a loose overhand knot (see Tying Knots). Slide the loop up the cord using the tip of a tapestry needle or beading awl until it lies behind the pearl.

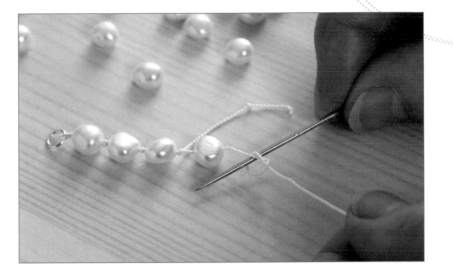

$4.$ Pull the cord through to tighten the knot so that it finishes snugly against the bottom of the pearl. Remove the needle at the last minute. Repeat until you have added sufficient pearls, stringing the last three without knots.

$5.$ Add another piece of gimp and a soldered ring or jump ring with clasp attached. Take the needle back down through the last pearl. Pull up to leave a little slack for the knots.

$6.$ Tie a half-hitch knot over the cord, take the needle through the next pearl and repeat the half-hitch knot. Take the needle through the next pearl and pull the cord taut and trim. This technique doesn't need glue to secure the knots.

design.
YOU WILL NEED:

- Green rutile quartz facetted pear drop briolettes, approx. 10 x 15mm – 20cm (8in) strand
- Green rutile quartz round 4–4.5mm – 38cm (15in) strand
- Hematite buttons 4–5mm diameter – 38cm (15in) strand
- Natural white nugget pearls 3–3.5mm – 38cm (15in) strand
- Silver-plated bead stringing wire, 49 strand, 0.46mm (0.018in)
- Two antique silver-plated bar ends with three loops
- Crimps, silver-plated, size 1, six
- Crimp covers, silver-plated, six
- Chain, antique silver-plated 64cm (25in)
- Silver-plated jump rings, four
- Silver-plated fastening
- Crimping pliers

Briolette Beauty

Faceted briolettes are one of the prettiest semi-precious beads and a crucial part of this necklace. This design uses a black and cream colour scheme but there are dozens of different semi-precious stones that you could use instead of the rutile quartz and hematite. Choose beads of a similar size and shape to replicate this

1. Cut one 30cm (16in) length and two 25cm (10in) lengths of bead stringing wire. Onto the longest strand pick up a pearl, a round quartz and a hematite. Pick up this bead sequence: hematite, round quartz, pearl, round quartz, hematite, round quartz, pearl, round quartz and then hematite.

2. Pick up a briolette so that the holes are towards the back. Add the bead sequence from step 1. Repeat four times then add a round quartz, hematite and a pearl. There should now be five briolettes evenly spaced on the strand.

3. On one of the shorter strands, pick up a pearl, round quartz, hematite, round quartz, pearl and round quartz, then the bead sequence. Pick up a briolette and a bead sequence. Repeat twice and then finish the strand to match the other end.

4. For the last strand, repeat step 3 but only repeat once to finish with two briolettes. Lay the strands out one under the other and check that the three lengths are attractively graduated when held together in a soft curve.

5. Pick up a crimp on the top strand of bead. Thread the bead stringing wire through the top loop of the bar end and then back through the crimp. Adjust to leave a short tail and then crimp with crimping pliers. Trim the tail.

6. Cover the crimp with a crimp cover. Squeeze the cover around the crimped wire until it resembles a round bead. Attach the other two wires in the same way. Push all the beads up against the crimp covers and then repeat at the other end to attach the other end bar.

7. Cut four 15cm (6in) lengths of chain. Attach two lengths to each bar end with a jump ring. Attach a jump ring to the end of both pairs of chains and a fastening to one of the jump rings. This necklace can only be worn in one direction so choose the clasp end depending on whether you are left or right-handed.

Semi-precious beads have tiny holes and so make sure the bead stringing wire (49 strands for a superior drape) fits through each bead.

Briar and Bramble Necklace

This stunning necklace could be made with all sorts of beads to create a completely different look. Changing the thong and chain to gold, copper or even a bright metallic colour with beads to match could change the style considerably. For a neat finish, make sure the bell cone ends fit snugly over the thong and chain at each end.

YOU WILL NEED:

- Bramble beads, 14mm, nine
- Green fluorite chips, 30cm (12in) string
- Silver-plated brass chain 2.5mm (⅛in) links x 3.5m (4yds)
- Silver leather cord 1mm x 3m (3¼yds)
- Silver-plated craft wire 0.315mm x 20cm (8in)
- Bright bead stringing wire, 19-strand, 0.46mm (0.018in)
- Silver-plated jump rings, 15
- Silver-plated eyepins, two
- Silver-plated trigger fastening
- Silver-plated bell cone ends, 10 x 20mm, two

1. Cut six 15cm (6in) lengths and six 15cm (5½in) lengths of chain. Lay the shorter lengths of chain centrally against three of the longer lengths and attach at each end with silver-plated jump rings so that the chains are parallel.

2. Cut six 45cm (17½in) lengths of silver leather thong and secure temporarily at one end by wrapping with fine wire. Feed the end of the four prepared chains onto the wire and wrap again to secure. Secure the wired end to the work surface with masking tape.

3. Use a mix of plaiting and knotting to create an attractive effect. Begin by dividing the bundle into three and plait, then tie the thong in an overhand knot over the jump rings, plaiting in between; tie a large knot in the centre as a focal point and again over the jump rings.

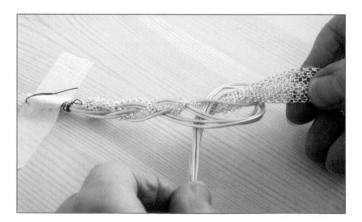

4. Continue to the other end. Secure the four chains again with fine wire then arrange the silver thong neatly and wrap to secure in a similar way to the other end. Trim the excess thong.

5. Cut two 38cm (15in) lengths of bead stringing wire. Secure the wire at one end of the necklace and feed through the chain and thong for about 2.5cm (1in). Pick up a few fluorite chips, then the 14mm bramble bead and add a few more fluorite chips.

6. Arrange the knotted and plaited chain in a bib shape on a microfibre beading mat. Thread the end of the bead stringing wire through the chain and leather to come out further up. Pick up more fluorite chips and the larger bead. Position the beads where you want them to lie and feed the tail through chain and thong again.

7. Continue adding bramble beads and fluorite chips on the wire until you reach the other end of the necklace. Repeat, using a second strand of bead stringing wire, adding beads to fill gaps and create a pleasing effect.

8. Feed a crimp bead onto the two strands of wire at each end and secure close to the end of the chains. Pick up a second crimp bead on both wires and secure, leaving a gap in between. Trim the beading wires and the leather cord.

9. Open the loop on an eyepin and attach to the gap between the crimps on the bead stringing wire. Feed the bell cone end over the eyepin and push down over the end of the necklace. Add a small bead if necessary and then make a plain loop on the end.

10. Check the length you would like the necklace to be and cut two approximately 30cm (12in) lengths of chain for each side. Attach one piece of chain to each loop. Adjust the length of these if necessary then use a jump ring to secure the ends of each pair together. Attach the lobster fastening to one jump ring and another jump ring to the other end.

Ice Cream Sundae Necklace

It may be difficult to get the exact beads used for this necklace but it is simply a string of beads with pretty flower bead dangles adding interest and texture. These flower beads are available in all sorts of colours and you can choose beads that match. String the beads on rattail, which can be finished neatly with tubular cord ends.

YOU WILL NEED:

- Tweed-covered beads, 20mm, coffee, three
- Satin-covered beads, 20mm, pink, three
- Ceramic beads, 12 x 16mm, two each in cream, mint and dark peach
- Ceramic spacers, 5 x 15cm, three each in cream and dark peach
- Ceramic beads, 6 x 8mm, four cream, five pink, three dark peach, three mint
- Donut spacer beads, 7 x 16mm, four silver
- Seed beads, size 6, five dark cream
- Pearl beads, 2.5mm, 30 ivory
- Flower beads, seven pink and eight mint
- Ivory rattail 2mm x 80cm
- Silver-plated or silver cord ends, i.d. 2mm, two
- Silver-plated lobster clasp
- Silver-plated jump ring
- Silver-plated headpins, two 5cm, 14 x 2.5cm
- Snipe- (chain-) nose pliers
- Round-nose pliers

1. To make each of the pink flowers into a bead dangle using the short headpins, pick up an ivory pearl bead, a flower bead and another pearl bead on the headpin. Trim the headpin to 7mm and bend over at a right-angle using snipe-nose pliers. Use round-nose pliers to bend the end of the headpin into a loop. Repeat with the remaining pink flowers and seven of the turquoise flower beads.

2. On one of the long headpins, pick up a pearl, a turquoise flower bead, a pearl, a size 6 seed bead, a small pink ceramic bead, a size 6 seed bead, a large, dark peach ceramic bead, then another size 6 seed bead and a pearl *. Trim the headpin to 7mm and bend over at right-angle using snipe-nose pliers. Use round-nose pliers to bend the end of the headpin into a loop.

3. To make a bead link, trim the flat end off the headpin and make an eyepin loop on one end. Pick up a size 6 seed bead, a satin-covered bead and another seed bead. Follow step 2 from*.

4. Join the large bead dangle to the bead link. Open three turquoise flower bead dangles and attach to the lower loop on the bead link. Repeat with three pink flower bead dangles.

5. Thread the rattail through the top loop of the bead link and drop down to the middle. Pick up beads, as shown, on either side of the bead dangle until you are ready to add some flower bead dangles.

6. Pick up one of each colour of flower bead dangle on each side and tie an overhand knot, so that the dangles are secured. You may need to guide the knot down using a 't' pin or large needle so that it is snug against the last large bead.

7. Add beads again to each side and add flower bead dangles in the same way. Continue adding beads, mixing shapes and colours until there is about 17–18cm (6¾–7in) of beads on each side. Finish with a small ceramic bead and tie a knot to secure the beads.

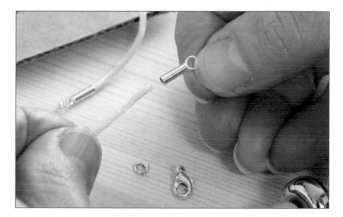

8. Check the length of the necklace then trim to suit. This design is 60cm (24in) long. Glue cord ends to each end and leave to dry. Attach a lobster clasp to one side using a jump ring.

Cosmic Links

The beauty of a piece of chain maille comes from perfectly formed jump rings linked together in a particular way, with each ring closed to create a perfect circle. For this reason it is essential not to skimp when buying the materials and choose saw cut jump rings so that the ends of each ring butt together exactly.

YOU WILL NEED:

• Sterling silver saw-cut jump rings, 400 – 1.02mm (19swg) i.d. 3.7mm

• Coloured wire approx. 8cm (3in)

• Magatamas, 100 x 4mm, jet black gloss

• Sterling silver fastening

• SWAROVSKI ELEMENTS Cosmic Ring Fancy Stone 4139 Jet 280, one 30mm, one 20mm

• Flat-nose pliers

1. If you are new to this technique, follow the steps for Byzantine chain, shown using coloured rings for clarity. Make a two in two chain using six of the sterling silver jump rings. Twist a piece of wire through the first two end rings so that you have something to hold.

2. Hold the twist tie between finger and thumb and *let the top two rings (5 and 6) fall down one on either side against rings 1 and 2. Hold rings 5 and 6 flat and the middle pair of rings (3 and 4) will be angled open into a knot formation.

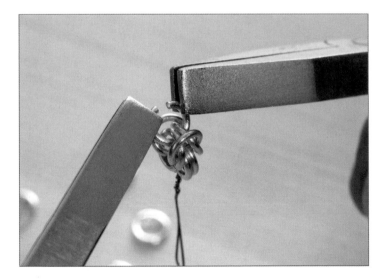

3. Add two more rings (7 and 8) through the top end of rings 5 and 6 to secure the knot formation of the Byzantine chain. Add two more pairs of rings (9 and 10 plus 11 and 12) to make the 2+2+2 sequence in step 1.

4. Fold back the last pair of rings (11 and 12) and hold them between finger and thumb as in step 2. Hold these rings flat and the middle (9 and 10) pair of rings in the sequence will be angled open again in a knot formation.

5. Add two more rings (13 and 14) through the top end of 11 and 12 to complete the double Byzantine unit. Add two more pairs of rings and repeat from * in step 2 to make a chain, ten double units long or about 13cm (5in).

6. To create the beaded sections of the Byzantine chain, pick up a magatama on a jump ring and insert the ring through the last pair of rings on the chain. Pick up another magatama and then close the ring. Add three more pairs of jump rings as a two in two chain between the magatamas.

7. Repeat from * in step 2 to make a double unit of Byzantine chain. Work ten of these Byzantine 'beads' joined with single jump rings, adding two magatamas to each single ring. Remove the twist of wire at the other end and add another ten Byzantine 'beads' joined with embellished single jump rings.

Use two pairs of blunt ended flat-nose pliers to minimise any damage as you join the rings.

8. Attach a silver trigger fastening to one end with a jump ring and then add a jump ring to the other end. Thread two cosmic rings or solid rings onto the necklace to finish.

Net and Rope Bracelet

Netting is a floppy tubular stitch which needs support to hold its tubular shape and so the rope, handmade to fit exactly, is not only a key design feature but also supports the bracelet down the centre. The beads can match the rope or contrast, so that the colour of the rope shows through the netting.

YOU WILL NEED:

• Toho seed beads, size 11 (2mm) in Ceylon custard (903), Ceylon apricot (904), galvanised matte rose gold (551F), transparent rainbow topaz (162C)

• Toho hexagons, size 11 (2mm) bronze (221)

• Toho magatamas, 3mm opaque oxblood (46)

• Kumihimo satin cord 1.5m (60in) of 2mm peach mix

• Gold end caps with fastening, 6mm internal diameter

• Size 10 beading needle

• Size D beading thread

• Beading mat

• Mandrel, 4.5mm (³⁄₁₆in) and 6mm (¼in) – optional

• Strong glue

• Rouleaux turner or long needle

1. For detailed step instructions on making tubular netting see the Tubular Netting techniques. Tip out a small quantity of Ceylon custard, Ceylon apricot and rose gold seed beads on the beading mat. Thread a needle with a 1.5m (1½yd) length of beading thread.

2. Pick up a Ceylon custard, Ceylon apricot, rose gold, then repeat the sequence until there are 15 seed beads on the thread. Tie in a circle leaving a 15cm (6in) tail. Take the needle through to the other side of the next rose gold (shared bead).

3. Pick up the following sequence of seed beads: CC, CA, RG, CA, CC, miss the next rose gold and take the needle through the next. Repeat until the netting is about 15cm (6in) long, stretched out. You may find it easier to support the netting on the smaller mandrel as you work. Sew in the thread ends securely using half-hitch knots.

4. To make the larger tubular netting, tip out a small quantity of topaz seed beads, hexagon beads and magatamas. Pick up a topaz seed bead, a bronze hexagon, a topaz seed bead and an oxblood magatama on a 1m (1yd) length of beading thread. Repeat the bead sequence four times (20 beads). Tie in a circle and take the needle through the next magatama.

5. Pick up this sequence: seed bead, hexagon, seed bead, magatama, seed bead, hexagon and seed bead; miss a magatama on the base circle and take the needle through the next magatama. Repeat until the netting is about 6cm (2⅜in) long. You can support the netting on the larger mandrel as you work. Sew in the thread ends securely using half-hitch knots (see Tying Knots).

6. Cut three 50cm (20in) lengths of satin cord. Secure the ends with fine wire or thread. Twist the ends in opposite directions until tightly twisted and then fold in half and let the rope twist up. Tie the cut ends together again.

7. Use a long needle or rouleaux turner to pull the rope through the middle of the netting tube. Sew the netting to the rope at each end. Thread the netting and rope through the shorter length of tubular netting. Leave it sitting in the middle. You can sew this in position if you prefer.

8. Check the length of the rope and decide where to wrap it with fine wire, prior to adding the end caps and fastening. Trim the rope close to the wire wrapping. Use a strong glue to stick the rope ends inside the caps. Leave to dry. If necessary, attach a fastening with jump rings.

Hana-Ami Earrings

Hana-Ami motifs always have the same number of beads but you can change the size by using larger or smaller beads. It is important to graduate the seed bead sizes as well as the focal beads so that the motifs remain flat. For these drop earrings, one of the larger XILIONS in the first two rounds is incorporated in the next smaller circle.

YOU WILL NEED:

• SWAROVSKI ELEMENTS
– XILION Bead 5328 Crystal Vitrail Medium (001 VM), 3mm x 22, 4mm x 10, 6mm x 12
– Crystal Round Pearl 5810 Tahitian-look (001 927) 4mm x 12, 6mm x 12

• Seed beads, matte iris teal (706): 36 each in size 15, size 11, size 8 F

• Fireline beading thread, size B, smoke

• Beading needle, size 12

• Silver-plated wire, 5cm (2in), 0.6mm (24 swg)

• Scissors

• Earring findings

1. If you are new to the technique, follow the detailed step instructions for Triangle Weave. Thread a fine beading needle with a 1m (1yd) length of beading thread. Pick up six size 6 seed beads and tie in a circle. Take the needle through the next two seed beads to hide the knot.

2. Pick up a 6mm crystal pearl, a size 8 seed bead, a 6mm XILION, a size 8 seed bead and a 6mm crystal pearl. Take the needle through the seed bead where the thread emerged again and through the next seed bead in the base circle.

3. Pick up a 6mm crystal pearl, a size 8 seed bead, a 6mm XILION and a size 8 seed bead. Take the needle through the third crystal pearl added, then the seed bead where the thread last emerged again and through the next seed bead in the base circle. Repeat to add the remaining four pearls.

4. Finish the Hana-Ami motif by picking up a size 6 seed bead, a 6mm XILION and another size 6 seed bead. Take the needle through the first and last pearls again. Take the needle around the outer seed beads and XILIONS to stabilize the motif, adding a half-hitch part way round. Bring the thread out of a XILION.

5. Pick up a size 11 seed bead, 4mm crystal pearl, a size 11 seed bead, 4mm crystal pearl and a size 11 seed bead. Take the needle through the 6mm XILION again and through the seed bead, crystal pearl and seed bead. Pick up five size 11 seed beads and circle through the original seed bead and all the seeds just added to form a circle. Pull the thread taut and take the needle through to come out one seed bead round from the original seed bead.

6. Complete this Hana-ami motif using size 11 seed beads and 4mm XILIONS and crystal pearls. Take the needle round the outside of the motif again to stabilize, coming out at one side of the top XILION. Pick up a 3mm XILION, a size 15 seed bead, a 3mm XILION and a size 15 seed bead. Take the needle through the top XILION from the previous motif and back through the next seed bead, XILION and seed bead.

7. Pick up five size 15 seed beads and circle through the original seed bead and all the seeds just added, to form a circle. Pull the thread taut and take the needle through to come out one seed bead round from the original seed bead.

8. Complete this Hana-ami motif using size 15 seed beads and 3mm XILIONS. Take the needle round the outside of the motif again to stabilize. Secure the thread by working one or two half-hitches coming out at one side of the top XILION. Make a second earring to match.

9. Cut a 5cm (2in) length of 0.6mm silver-plated wire. Pass the wire through the top XILION on the earring. Make a wrapped loop as though this was a briolette or pendant bead. Attach an earring finding and complete the other earring to match.

Deep Pool Ring

The beads that you choose for stitching a bezel are quite crucial to the finished effect as it is important to enhance the SWAROVSKI ELEMENTS Square Fancy Stone in the centre. This design uses top quality seed beads with unusual textures, such as Toho triangles and charlottes that reflect the light in different ways.

YOU WILL NEED:

- SWAROVSKI ELEMENTS Square Fancy Stone 4470 indicolite (379) 12 x 12mm
- Toho triangle crystal prairie green (270), size 11 (2mm)
- Delicas, galvanised turquoise (415), size 15
- Charlotte Japanese seed beads, silver, size 15
- Charlotte Czech seed beads, crystal AB, size 15
- Size D thread (S-Lon or Fireline), 1.5m (1½yd)
- Ring base
- Epoxy resin glue

1. Pick up 20 triangle beads on a 1.5m (1½yd) length of thread, tie in circle leaving a 15cm (6in) tail and then pass the needle through a few beads ready to work circular peyote stitch. Pick up a triangle bead, miss a bead and pass through the next bead along. Continue all the way round, remembering to step up through two beads at the end of the round.

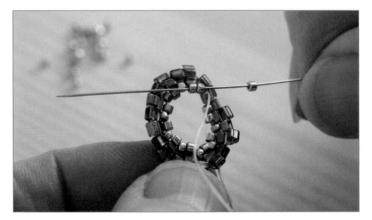

2. Add another round of triangle beads. Work a round of silver Japanese charlottes, a round of turquoise Delicas and finally a round of clear AB Czech charlottes. Pull the thread taut as you work and then take the needle through beads to come out at the other side of the bezel between two triangle beads.

3. Insert the square stone face down in the bezel and repeat step 2 to secure the stone inside. Secure the thread with a half-hitch knot (see Tying Knots) then take the needle through the beads to come out in the centre row of triangles at the edge of the bezel.

4. To begin the herringbone stitch, pick up two Delicas, miss the next pair of triangle beads and pass the needle through the next triangle bead along. Pull the thread taut so that the Delica beads are sitting almost side by side in a 'v' shape. Repeat all the way round. Step up through the first Delica again ready to begin the next round.

5. * Pick up two Delicas and go down through the second Delica added in the previous round. Pick up a silver charlotte and go up through the next Delica along. Repeat from * until you have completed the round. Step up through two Delicas to begin the next round.

6. Begin to add more silver charlottes using peyote stitch, as shown in Working a Frilled Collar. Work the first herringbone stitch then pick up a silver charlotte, pass the needle through the charlotte from the last round and pick up another charlotte.

7. Take the needle through the next Delica ready to work the next herringbone stitch. Continue all the way round and step up through two Delicas. On the next round add three charlottes in peyote stitch, and then four charlottes in the following round. Push all the silver peyote stitch sections forwards to shape the ring.

8. In the final round you will be embellishing the tips of herringbone stitch. After stepping up through two Delicas, pick up a Delica, a silver charlotte and another Delica. Go down through the next Delica and work peyote stitch, adding five silver charlottes before the next herringbone stitch. Pull the thread taut as you go.

When stitching bezels with tiny beads it helps to condition the thread before you begin as the wax helps keep the thread from slipping back through the bead after each stitch.

9. Work all the way round to complete the funky star-shaped ring. Sew in the thread ends using half-hitch knots to secure. Trim the ends neatly. Secure a ring base to the reverse side using epoxy resin glue.

YOU WILL NEED:

- Silk dupion, 25 x 30cm (10 x 12in)
- Lacy's Stiff Stuff, 11 x 14cm (4¼ x 5½in)
- Thin wadding, 11 x 14cm (4¼ x 5½in)
- Silver-lined purple bugles, 12mm x 50 and 6mm x 55
- Seed beads, size 11 (2mm), Ceylon custard, Ceylon apricot, galvanised matte rose gold, silver-lined deep pink, 5g each
- Seed beads, size 8, silver-lined pale pink, 5g
- Seed beads, size 6, pink-lined Ceylon ivory, 5g
- Selection of 6mm facetted beads in opaque lilac, opaque custard yellow, lilac, amethyst and pink (approx. seven each)
- Round pearlised glass bead, 6mm, eight
- Tacking thread
- Sewing thread to match silk
- Strong beading thread such as Power Pro
- Organza ribbon, 1.25m (50in) of 12mm (½in)
- Ribbon crimp ends, 12mm (½in), two
- Fastening
- Jump rings, two
- Jewellery glue

Bead Encrusted Bib

Bib-style necklaces stormed onto the fashion scene a few years ago and are so flattering that they are definitely here to stay. This elegantly shaped design echoes the décolletage and is particularly stylish. Although you want a few highlights, the beads should be of a similar density of hue so they blend together well.

1. Draw a rectangle 15 x 7.5cm (6 x 3in) and then draw the shape of the bib necklace and cut out. Use this to cut a piece of thin wadding and Lacy's Stiff Stuff.

2. Lay the template on the reverse side of a 25 x 15cm (10 x 6in) piece of silk dupion and mark around the edge with a pencil or embroidery marker. Tack along the line. Lay the fabric face down and position the wadding and then the Lacy's Stiff Stuff on top. Sew a few large backstitches with tacking thread to secure temporarily.

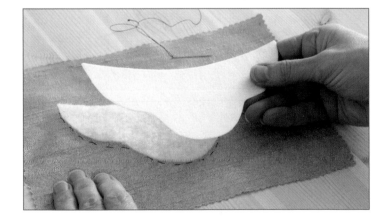

3. Secure a double length of beading thread on the reverse side at the centre near the bottom edge. Bring the thread through to the right side so that it emerges just above the tacking line in the centre. Pick up a short bugle and lay flat where you want it to sit. Take the needle back through, close to the top of the bugle. Continue working around the edge, adding another 12 bugles. You will need to open tiny gaps on the outer edge so that the bugles follow the shape of the bib.

4. Add 15 larger bugles, keeping them side-by-side on the outer edge and fanned out slightly to go around the concave curve. Add about 15 short bugles and then finish the side edge with the long bugles again. Sew in the thread end securely. Join on a new double thread in the bottom centre and complete the other side in the same way.

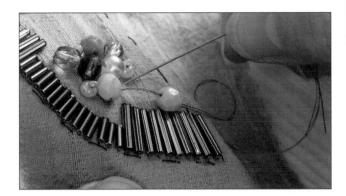

5. Arrange five clusters of the 6mm beads on the bib, making each cluster slightly different. Lift off and then stitch each bead down with a single stitch.

6. Begin to fill in the background with seed beads. Use the Ceylon apricot and custard mainly and then add the occasional galvanised matte rose gold and silver-lined deep pink. Add a size 8 silver-lined pale pink from time to time to add a bit of sparkle. These beads are all added with a single stitch as above. The larger size 6 seed beads are added as a stack. Take the needle through large beads twice to make them more secure.

7. Once the background is filled, remove the tacking thread. Trim the fabric around the edge to 1.5cm (⅝in). Notch or snip around the edge of the bib (not too close to the embroidery). Sew from side to side using strong thread to secure the seam allowances on the reverse side.

8. Tack the outline of the bib on the second piece of silk dupion. Notch and snip around the edge and turn under, so it is slightly smaller than the embroidered bib. Tack or press around the edge. Lay the backing on the reverse side and pin.

9. Cut the ribbon in half. Fold each piece in half and tuck under the backing at each edge. Sew the backing in place with slip or over-sewing stitches.

10. Check the length of the necklace and adjust the ribbon length if required. Attach the ribbon crimps, adding a little jewellery glue for extra security. Add a jump ring to each ribbon crimp end and then attach a fastening.

Feather and Fabric Brooch

Use a variety of line bead embroidery techniques to create different textures on this pretty brooch. The design is worked directly into a felt backing so you could make it any shape you want, then add a backing and brooch back. The design combines many different elements with well coordinated colours.

YOU WILL NEED:

- Black felt, 13 x 5cm (5 x 2in)
- Pale pink organza scrap
- Pale pink tulle scrap
- SWAROVSKI ELEMENTS
  – XILION beads 5328, rose (209) 3mm x 10
  – Round bead 5000, fuchsia (243 4mm x 9
  – Oval Fancy Stone, 4120, light rose (223) 18 x 13mm,
  – Square, Fancy Stone 4470, rose alabaster (293) 12mm
- Japanese charlotte seed beads, silver, size 15
- Square sequins, black iris finish, 5mm (¼in), 10
- Black feathers
- Silver-plated chain, 8cm (3in)
- Large kilt pin, 7.5cm (3in)

1. Trim the corners of the black felt to round them off. Cut a 14cm (5½in) circle from pink organza, fold in half and sew small running stitches along the raw edge. Pull the semi-circle up so that the stitched edge is less than 5cm (2in).

2. Pin the organza to the reverse side at the bottom so that 1–2cm (½–¾in) is jutting out below. Tuck the tops of about four black feathers between the organza and the felt. Stitch through all the layers to secure the feathers and organza.

3. Cut roughly a 6cm (2½in) square piece of pink tulle. Wrap around the oval stone and then stitch in the bottom right corner of the felt. Work a row of chain stitch with silver charlotte seed beads, following the curve of the oval stone.

4. Sew one end of the silver-plated chain to the edge of the felt beside the double line of charlotte seed beads. Trim to length and then sew to the felt.

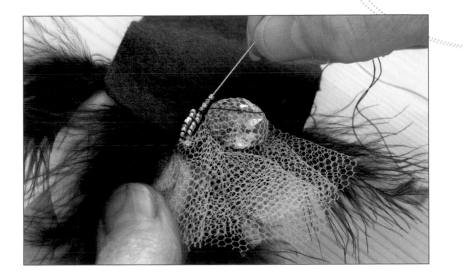

5. Wrap the square stone in a smaller piece of pink tulle and sew to the left side of the felt. Stitch two rows of chain stitch above the square stone, following the gentle curve of the stone.

6. Continue adding curved rows to the left side: add a row of square sequins along the top edge of the charlotte seed beads then add another row of charlottes with chain stitch. Sew another length of chain across the top of the beads. Add a row of round crystals by couching then finish with a line of chain stitch.

7. Change back to the right side, adding a row of chain stitch, a row of sequins and a row of chain stitch. Sew the rose XILIONS using couching and then add another piece of chain to finish. Sew in the ends securely.

8. Fold the felt over the kilt pin. Sew around the edges with tiny stab stitches through all layers to hide all the raw ends and to secure the pin.

Bead Details

The details of specific beads used in the Projects chapter are listed below. Those beads without a shop reference are either fashion beads without precise details or basic beads, generally available from your local bead shop.

JUICY PEARLS
Glass pearls (Bead Crazy)
Brass wire (Bead Sisters)

CRYSTAL STATEMENT
SWAROVSKI ELEMENTS (E-Beads)
SWAROVSKI settings (E-Beads)
Ring base (Bead Crazy)

PEARL BRACELET
Fresh water pearls
Silk cord
(all Precious Sparkle Beads)

BRIOLETTE BEAUTY
Green Rutile Quartz briolettes and round
Hematite buttons
Natural white nugget pearls
(all Precious Sparkle Beads)

BRIAR AND BRAMBLE
Green fluorite chips (Precious Sparkle Beads)
Bramble beads (Bead Crazy)
Brass silver-plated chain (E-Beads)
Silver leather cord (E-Beads)

ICE CREAM SUNDAE
Beads from a selection (Bead Crazy)

COSMIC LINKS
SWAROVSKI ELEMENTS (E-Beads)
Magatamas (Stitch'n' Craft)
Sterling silver jump rings (Bead Sisters)

Toho seed beads
Toho hexagons
Toho magatamas
Kumihimo satin cord
(all E-Beads)

NET AND ROPE BRACELET
Toho seed beads
Toho hexagons
Toho magatamas
Kunihimo satin cord
(all E-Beads)

HANA-AMI EARRINGS
SWAROVSKI ELEMENTS (E-Beads)
Toho seed beads (E-Beads)

DEEP POOL RING
SWAROVSKI ELEMENTS (E-Beads)
Toho triangles (E-Beads)
Delicas (Spellbound Beads)
Charlottes (Edinburgh Bead Shop)

BEAD ENCRUSTED BIB
Toho seed beads (E-Beads)
6mm facetted beads (Bead Crazy)
Lacy's Stiff Stuff (Edinburgh Bead Shop)

FEATHER AND FABRIC BROOCH
SWAROVSKI ELEMENTS (E-beads)
Charlottes (Edinburgh Bead Shop)

Crystal Statement Ring Diagram

Suppliers

UK AND EUROPE

E-Beads Ltd
Unit TR1-2
Trowbray House
108 Weston Street
London
SE1 3QB
Tel: 0207 367 6217
Email: via website
UK: www.e-beads.co.uk
EU: www.i-beads.eu
DE: www.i-perlen.de
FR: www.i-perles.fr
AT: www.iperlen.at
BE: www.i-perles.be

Bead Crazy
55 George Street
Perth
PH1 5LB
Tel: 01738 442 288
Email: info@beadcrazy.co.uk
www.beadcrazy.co.uk

Bead Sisters
Tel: 01776 830 352
Email: sales@beadsisters.co.uk
www.beadsisters.co.uk

Edinburgh Bead Shop
6 Dean Park Street
Stockbridge
Edinburgh
EH4 1JW
Tel: 01313 433 222
Email: info@beadshopedinburgh.co.uk
www.beadshopscotland.co.uk

Jencel
30 Lees Hall Avenue
Sheffield
S8 9JE

Tel: 01142 509 565
Email: celia@jencel.co.uk
www.jencel.co.uk

Palmer Metals
401 Broad Lane
Coventry
CV5 7AY
Tel: 0845 644 9343
Email: sales@palmermetals.co.uk
www.palmermetals.co.uk

Stitch'n'craft
2 Chaldicott Barns
Tokes Lane
Semley
Dorset
SP7 9AW
Tel: 01747 830 666

Jilly Beads
Tel: 01524 412 728
Email: query@jillybeads.co.uk
www.jillybeads.co.uk

The Bead shop (Nottingham)
7 Market Street
Nottingham
NG1 6HY
Tel: 01159 588 903
info@mailorderbeads.co.uk
www.mailorderbeads.co.uk

Precious Sparkle Beads
8 Bridge Lane
Perth
PH1 5JJ
Email: info@precioussparklebeads.co.uk
www.precioussparklebeads.co.uk

USA

Firemountain Gems
1 Firemountain Way
Grants Pass
OR 97526-2373
Tel: 800 423 2319
Email: questions@firemtn.com
www.firemountain.com

Land of Odds
718 Thomson Lane
Ste 123
Nashville
TN 37204
Tel: 615 292 0610
Email: oddsian@landofodds.com
www.landofodds.com

Out on a Whim
121 E. Eotali Avenue
Cotati
CA 94931
Tel: 800 232 3111
Email: whimbeads.com
www.whimbeads.com

The Beadin' Path
15 Main Street
Freeport
ME 04032
Tel: 207 865 4785
Email: beads@beadinpath.com
www.beadinpath.com

Acknowledgements

The Publishers: Thanks are owed to E-Beads Limited in particular Anastasia and Kelly Yau for their support and guidance; visit www.e-beads.co.uk for an excellent online shopping experience browsable in English, French and German. Thanks also to SWAROVSKI ELEMENTS for their support and for providing some of the crystals used.

Dorothy Wood: I'm delighted to have had the opportunity to write *The Bead Jewellery Bible*, The best selling *The Beader's Bible* has been such a success and this new bible focusing on jewellery was a new and most enjoyable challenge. Thanks to E-Beads, Palmer Metals, Bead Sisters and Precious Sparkle Beads who have all been so generous supplying beads and materials for the book. Thanks to Cheryl Brown and the team at David and Charles for their support and expertise putting the book together, to Cathy Joseph for editing the manuscript so adeptly and to Simon Whitmore for the fabulous photography which shows the projects so beautifully and for the new step-by-step shots that make such a difference to a technical book.

Index